one-pot cooking

one-pot cooking

Sarah Edmonds

Photography by Thomas Odulate

southwater

This edition is published by Southwater

Southwater is an imprint of
Anness Publishing Limited
Hermes House
88–89 Blackfriars Road
London SE1 8HA
tel. 020 7401 2077
fax 020 7633 9499

Distributed in the USA by
Anness Publishing Inc.
27 West 20th Street
Suite 504
New York
NY 10011
tel. 212 807 6739
fax 212 807 6813

Distributed in the UK by
The Manning Partnership
251–253 London Road East
Batheaston
Bath BA1 7RL
tel. 01225 852 727
fax 01225 852 852

Distributed in Australia by
Sandstone Publishing
Unit 1
360 Norton Street
Leichhardt
New South Wales 2040
tel. 02 9560 7888
fax 02 9560 7488

1 3 5 7 9 10 8 6 4 2

Publisher: Joanna Lorenz
Project Editor: Zoe Antoniou
Designer: Joyce Chester
Photographers: Karl Adamson, Edward Allwright, David Armstrong, James Duncan, Michelle Garrett, Amanda Heywood, Janine Hosegood, David Jordan, William Lingwood, Patrick McLeavey, Michael Michaels, Thomas Odulate and Juliet Piddington.
Recipes: Kit Chan, Frances Cleary, Roz Denny, Matthew Drennan, Sarah Edmonds, Rafi Fernandez, Silvana Franco, Shirley Gill, Rosamund Grant, Janine Hosegood, Deh-Ta Hsiung, Shehzad Husain, Peter Jordan, Manisha Kanani, Soheila Kimberley, Masaki Ko, Ruby Le Bois, Lesley Mackley, Norman MacMillan, Sue Maggs, Sallie Morris, Elisabeth Lambert Ortiz, Maggie Pannell, Anne Sheasby, Liz Trigg and Steven Wheeler.
Stylists: Madeleine Brehaut, Elizabeth Wolf Cohen, Clare Hunt, Maria Kelly, Marion McLornan, Blake Minton and Marion Price.
Food for photography: Jacqueline Clark, Joanne Craig, Katherine Hawkins, Jane Stevenson, Carol Tennant and Judy Williams.

For all recipes, quantities are given in both metric and imperial measures and, where appropriate, measures are also given in standard cups and spoons. Follow one set, but not a mixture, because they are not interchangeable.

Please use medium-sized eggs unless otherwise stated.

Picture on p7 shows (clockwise from top): wild rice, black glutinous rice, Japanese rice, Camargue red rice, Thai fragrant rice, white glutinous rice and long grain with wild rice (centre).

Previously published as *Step-by-step 50 Classic Rice Recipes*

CONTENTS

INTRODUCTION

Mention one-pot cooking and everyone's eyes light up! Immediate thoughts are of warming comfort-food, easy preparation, minimal washing up and wonderful pans bubbling to the brim with delicious rich stews.

All true, but the art of one-pot cooking goes much further. In this book we return to some basic cookery methods; braising, stir-frying, poaching and boiling. They may sound rather mundane but, with imagination and the amazingly wide range of ingredients available now, these techniques take on a new lease of life, giving us some of the most exciting flavours we've experienced for a long time.

Browse through the soup chapter and you'll find a recipe for every occasion. Immediately, you'll be able to see how easy they are to make and, with the addition of herbs, spices and unusual ingredients, how delicious and exciting they can be.

Stews and Pot-roasts are not necessarily the heavy dishes you may imagine: some are light and fresh, according to the season. There are delicious recipes for pasta, grains, noodles, stir-fries and sautés to provide you with endless ideas for family meals and casual entertaining. Jambalaya and Risotto are year-round hits and Lemon Couscous Salad is perfect for summer entertaining, while the vegetarian chapter includes tasty recipes suitable for all the family.

The recipes will become firm favourites for quick lunches, informal evening meals or more sophisticated dinner parties.

Herbs and Spices

Use fresh herbs whenever possible; if you have to
substitute dried herbs, use only about half the
quantity as they have a more concentrated flavour.
Dried herbs and spices should be stored in a cool,
dark, dry place.

Bouquet Garni

Used to flavour soups and
casseroles, a bouquet garni is
usually a combination of thyme,
parsley and a bay leaf, sometimes
with a piece of leek or celery and
black peppercorns. Buy ready-
prepared bouquets, packed in
small sachets resembling tea bags,
or tie your own in muslin.
Remove before serving. (1)

Caraway Seeds

These small brown seeds have
a slightly bitter, but warm,
aniseed flavour. They are used
extensively in Central European
cookery in both sweet and
savoury dishes, such as goulash,
sauerkraut, cakes and biscuits.
The flavour of caraway seeds
goes particularly well with
potatoes, onions and cheese. (2)

Chillies, Chilli Powder and Crushed Chillies

There are many varieties of fresh
chillies. As a general rule, the
larger, fleshier chillies are milder
than the small, thin, slightly
wrinkled-looking ones. To reduce
the heat, remove the seeds.

Chilli powders come in varying
strengths: make sure you read the
label carefully! Most are a blend
of ground chillies with other
herbs and spices (often oregano
and cumin seeds); others can be
pure ground chilli and very hot.

Crushed chillies make an
excellent garnish for rice, noodle
and egg dishes. (3)

Coriander Leaf, Coriander Seeds and Ground Coriander

Quickly becoming one of the
most popular flavours in cookery,
coriander leaf has a distinct
aroma and a wonderful spicy,
earthy, peppery taste. It's an
excellent addition to meat, fish
and vegetable dishes. Add
towards the end of cooking, or
sprinkle over the finished dish
for maximum flavour.

From the same plant, but not
interchangeable with coriander
leaf, the seeds, whole or ground,
have a much spicier flavour, with
a distinct hint of orange peel.
Ground coriander is an essential
ingredient of curry powder and it
can also be found in many
Moroccan-style, spicy meat and
vegetable stews. (4)

Cumin and Cumin Seeds

This is another spice that goes
well with meat, fish, vegetables,
and cheese. It has a srong
aromatic, slightly bitter flavour.
Ground cumin is often coupled
with ground coriander. (5)

Dill Weed

The light, feathery leaves make a
lovely garnish and dill's fresh,
sweet, slightly aniseed flavour is a
subtle accompaniment to fish,
chicken and egg dishes. It is also
excellent in cream sauces. Be
careful not to overpower dill's
delicate flavour. Add dill towards
the end of cooking for the
maximum flavour. (6)

Ginger (Fresh Root and Ground)

Used more and more in recent
years, ginger's warm, sweet,
spicy flavour adds a kick to any
recipe, but tastes particularly
good in seafood and chicken
dishes. When buying fresh root
ginger, look for smooth plump
roots. Store the unpeeled root,
tightly wrapped, in the fridge for
up to 6 weeks or so. If
substituting ground ginger in a
recipe, 5 ml/1 tsp is roughly
equivalent to a 2.5 cm/1 in piece
of fresh root ginger. (7)

Juniper Berries

These small, dark berries give
their bitter-sweet pine flavour to
gin. They are a perfect partner
for richly flavoured meats and
game and can also be used in
sweet dishes. Crush the berries
lightly before use, to release their
flavour. (8)

Kaffir Lime Leaves

These aromatic leaves add their
unmistakable flavour to many
Indonesian and Thai dishes.
Distinctive in appearance, kaffir
lime leaves are dark green, shiny,
and joined in pairs, forming a
figure-of-eight shape. The leaves
freeze well so, if you find a
supply, buy plenty and store
them in the freezer wrapped in
polythene. Add the leaves whole
and remove them before eating
or finely chop the leaves and
incorporate them in the dish. (9)

Lemon Grass

This is a strange-looking root
with a wonderful aromatic lemon
flavour. Finely chop or slice the
base of the root, or use the
coarse stems whole and remove
them before serving. If you can't
find lemon grass, use a little
lemon rind instead. (10)

Oregano

Oregano grows wild and has a
distinctive, strong, pungent
flavour. You'll recognise it in
many Italian dishes, including
pizzas. It is also known as wild
marjoram. Marjoram is cultivated
and can be used in oregano's
place, though it has a more
delicate flavour. (11)

Turmeric

Mildly aromatic with a slight
pepper and ginger hint, turmeric
is a superb vivid yellow colour.
This spice is often used to colour
and flavour rice and pickles and
is an essential ingredient in curry
powder. (12)

Storecupboard Ingredients

Most of the recipes call for fresh produce, but many also make use of canned or bottled ingredients. Most of us have the basics, but here are a few suggestions for useful additions to your storecupboard.

Anchovy Fillets
Canned anchovies are imported from the Mediterranean. They've been filleted and salted before being packed in oil. A little goes a long way, so use sparingly. To reduce their saltiness, soak them in a little water or milk and rinse. Add finely chopped anchovies to salads and pasta dishes or pound them to a paste and use in dressings or stir-fries. (1)

Balsamic Vinegar
This is made in the Modena region of northern Italy. It has a rich, dark colour and a sweet-sour flavour. Some balsamic vinegar is aged for 15–20 years and really should be savoured as a dressing. Buy a slightly cheaper, younger vinegar for cooking; it still gives an excellent flavour. In Modena, balsamic vinegar is used to dress strawberries: this traditional dish is easily prepared by sprinkling a little vinegar over sliced strawberries, then leaving them to stand for 30 minutes before serving. (2)

Capers
The full, unopened buds of the caper bush are picked and preserved in vinegar. They have quite a sharp flavour and need only be used in small quantities. Store in the fridge, submerged in their liquid, after opening. Capers are used extensively in Mediterranean cooking. (3)

Oils
There are many oils to choose from, all with different characteristics and uses. Some are more suited to salad dressings, others are better used for cooking or marinating foods.

Sunflower Oil
Sunflower oil (4), which is light and tasteless, is an ideal all-round oil for cooking. It can also be mixed with other highly flavoured oils to dilute their strength.

Olive Oil
Extra virgin olive oil is considered the best with a maximum acidity of 1 per cent. Less expensive oils, from third or fourth pressings of the olives, will usually be slightly more acidic. Use extra virgin olive oil (5) for salad dressings – drizzling it over foods for a rich olive flavour – for sauces and for dressing pasta. Keep a slightly cheaper olive oil (6) for cooking and marinating.

Sesame Oil
A strongly flavoured oil, such as sesame, is an ideal storecupboard ingredient (7). Just a few drops give a wonderful flavour to noodles, pasta and stir-fries and it also makes a great addition to marinades. Cook it gently or add it at the end of cooking as sesame oil burns at a low temperature.

Passata
An Italian favourite, passata is a relatively new product on the supermarket shelves, but every storecupboard should have a jar! Used instead of canned tomatoes, it's made from puréed and sieved tomatoes and it makes a wonderfully smooth and flavoursome base for all kinds of sauces, casseroles, soups and pasta sauces. (8)

Pine Nuts
These are the seeds collected from pine trees, such as the stone pine. The small soft oval kernel has a unique flavour, which is improved by toasting before use. Pine nuts make great additions to salads, stuffings and stews and are one of the essential ingredients of pesto sauce. They have a high fat content, so don't keep them very long or they will become rancid: buy them in small quantities and use them quickly. (9)

Soy Sauce
Made from fermented soya beans, soy sauce is available in dark and light varieties. Light soy (10) should be used if only a hint of soy flavour is required and very little colour. Dark soy (11) has a stronger, sweeter flavour and should be used for spicier dishes that require more robust seasoning. Remember that soy sauce is quite salty, so add extra salt sparingly.

Sun-dried Tomatoes and Sun-dried Tomato Paste
These dried tomatoes are sold either preserved in olive oil or dry; the latter need to be soaked before use. The rich, strong flavour lifts any salad, stuffing, soup or stew (12). Sun-dried tomato paste is the puréed form and it adds a much fuller flavour than ordinary tomato purée. Add to sauces, casseroles and baked pasta dishes. (13)

Tabasco Sauce
This is a fiery-hot sauce, made in Louisiana from chillies. Add it to food at the table for extra spice, or use to flavour soups, stews and sauces. Add a little at a time: it's easier to add more than to take it away! (14)

Unusual Ingredients

Some of the recipes call for slightly more unusual ingredients, items you may not already have in stock. It's certainly worth hunting for these; most supermarkets should stock them.

Chorizo
This spicy sausage from Spain has a coarse, meaty texture and full flavour. It's made from pork and paprika, which gives it its wonderful colour. You can buy raw chorizo (1), which is similar in size to a standard sausage; you may also find ready-to-eat sausage, sliced like salami. (2)

Canned Coconut Milk (3) and Creamed Coconut (4)
Often used in oriental cooking, both versions add a creamy texture and mild coconut flavour. Most supermarkets stock blocks of creamed coconut, which is reconstituted with boiling water to the consistency you need, usually that of single cream.

Crème Fraîche
This delicious, thick cream, used extensively in French cooking, has a slightly sour taste, which is perfect in soups and casseroles, over pasta and in sauces. If you can't buy crème fraîche, use equal amounts of thick double and soured cream, mixed lightly together. (5)

Dried Porcini Mushrooms
Dried mushrooms make a tasty addition to risottos, soups and casseroles. Just a few will enrich and add a strong mushroom flavour. Dried mushrooms need to be reconstituted before use. However, don't waste the liquid they're soaked in: use it as a flavourful stock. (6)

Thai Fish Sauce
One of the main flavours of Thai cooking, Thai fish sauce is a thin, brown liquid extracted from salted, fermented fish. Use sparingly; you can always add more if you like the flavour. It is quite salty, so taste the dish before you add any extra salt. (7)

Hoisin Sauce

An essential ingredient for oriental dishes, this is a rich, dark sauce, made from soya bean paste, garlic, vinegar, spices and sugars. It gives a wonderful sweet, yet spicy, flavour to poultry, meat and stir-fries and can also be used as a glaze or sauce for poultry and meat. (8)

Oyster Sauce

Although it is made from oysters, soy sauce, spices and seasonings, this sauce doesn't taste salty or fishy, but is rich and savoury. Oyster sauce is a perfect partner for meat, fish and vegetables and can be used as a dipping sauce or to flavour stir-fries. (9)

Plum Sauce

A smooth, dark red-brown sauce made from plums preserved with chilli, ginger, spices, vinegar and sugar. It also makes a great addition to stir-fries and marinades, or can be used as a dipping sauce. (10)

Pumpkin and Squash

You'll be familiar with pumpkin (11) but it's only available for a limited time each year. Most supermarkets stock butternut squash (12) and kabocha squash (13), which can be substituted for pumpkin in recipes. Pumpkin and squash are delicious on their own, but can also be added to soups and stews. They are tender and slightly nutty and go well with spices, such as cumin, coriander, ginger or nutmeg.

Tahini

A pale, smooth and oily paste made from ground raw sesame seeds. It is used to flavour humous, but can also be used to give a sesame nut flavour to dips, casseroles and soups. (14)

Tofu

Also known as beancurd, tofu is made from soya beans which, when puréed with water, can be strained to form a milk. A solidifying agent is added to the milk and the resulting curds are pressed. Tofu has little flavour itself but soaks up other flavours readily, so is ideal for stir-fries and desserts. Store in the fridge, covered in water. Change the water daily and it will keep for about five days. Tofu has a high protein content and is suitable for vegetarians. (15)

Water Chestnuts

White, crunchy vegetables with a juicy, sweet flavour, water chestnuts are available in cans. Drain off all the liquid and add whole or sliced. They can be eaten raw and stay crunchy when cooked. (16)

Pasta, Noodles, Grains and Pulses

More and more types of pasta and noodles are appearing in shops and supermarkets, and there is such a wide range of pulses that the choice can be daunting. Here is a selection of ones you'll find in the recipes.

Pasta

Always choose the best you can afford. Pasta made with durum wheat and egg has a better, richer flavour. Dried pasta has improved so much that fresh is no longer necessarily better. Experiment with different brands and find one you like.

Choose a pasta suitable for the sauce: long thin noodles (1) and spaghetti (2) are better with lighter sauces, such as olive oil dressings. Thicker sauces need a pasta shape that will trap sauce in its grooves and folds. (3)

Cook pasta in plenty of boiling salted water, stirring occasionally with a fork to prevent it from sticking. Test regularly until cooked *al dente* (tender but slightly firm to the bite). Drain and return to the warm pan. Allow a little water to cling to the pasta, to prevent it from drying out and sticking together. Add the sauce and serve immediately.

Egg Noodles

Used in oriental cooking for soups, stir-fries or with sauces, and richer than pasta, these are excellent with soy- and sesame-based sauces. Most dried egg noodles are dried medium or thin and are sold in compressed, flat rectangles. Simply pour over boiling water and allow to stand before using. (4)

Rice Noodles

Made from rice flour and water, ribbon noodles (5) can be bought in a variety of widths. Authentic rice noodles are available from oriental, Thai and other specialist food shops. The noodles need to be soaked in boiling water before use in stir-fries and other oriental dishes.

Arborio Rice

Essential for a perfect risotto, it has shorter, rounder grains than long grain rice, with slightly translucent edges and a white, hard core. Arborio rice can absorb a lot of cooking liquid without becoming too soft, giving risotto its characteristic creamy texture but with a slight bite. (6)

Couscous

Made from semolina grains, which are treated and coated with a fine wheat flour, couscous simply needs moistening, allowing the grains to swell and soften. The couscous can then be used or steamed and served piping hot. (7)

Pearl Barley

Pearl barley is the polished and refined form of the whole grain, which means it cooks more quickly. It can be added to soups and casseroles to enrich and thicken them. (8)

Chick-peas

These pale golden peas, which look rather like hazelnuts, are an essential ingredient of humous, a Greek dip of chick-peas, ground sesame paste, garlic and olive oil. They make a wonderful addition to soups and stews, giving a rich, nutty flavour. The dried peas (9) need lengthy soaking and cooking. Canned chick-peas make an excellent substitute. (10)

Red Kidney Beans

Probably the most well known, and frequently used beans, they retain their wonderful red colour on cooking. The canned variety makes an excellent addition to the storecupboard. Drain and rinse well before use. (11)

Cannellini Beans

These creamy-white, slender beans have a fluffy texture and buttery flavour and are excellent in salads, soups and stews. Again, canned varieties are good. Use haricot beans if you can't buy cannellini beans. (12) and (13)

Black-eyed Beans

Attractive, pale-coloured beans with a black patch where they were joined to the pod, these have a wonderful creamy flavour and add great colour and texture to a dish. Try them in salads, stews and curries. (14)

Flageolet Beans

These are pale green coloured beans, with a fresh, subtle flavour that shouldn't be overpowered by using too many spices and strong flavours. They are a variety of the haricot bean family and are harvested before they are ripe, these are the most delicate of all pulses. Toss cooked flageolet beans in olive oil or butter and serve them as an accompaniment to lamb or chicken. Alternatively, add them to a mixed bean salad, tossed in a simple French dressing. They also make a great supper dish, cooked with plenty of onions, bacon and lemon, then seasoned well and served with crusty bread. (15)

Equipment

The right equipment makes cooking so much easier. Our guide helps you to decide whether you have all you require in your kitchen, or need to invest in some new equipment.

Choosing Pans for One-Pot Cookery

It is important to buy the best pans you can afford; they'll definitely last a lot longer. Thin, flimsy pans burn quickly and scorch the contents and it can be difficult to maintain a constant temperature in them.

For soups, stews and pot-roasts, always make sure the pan is big enough (1). Too small, and the pan may overflow or the ingredients may be packed so tightly that it could increase the cooking time. Too big, and a lot of the liquid will evaporate, causing the dish to dry out. Remember to check in the recipe whether the dish will need to go in the oven to finish cooking; if so, a flameproof casserole (2) may be more suitable than a saucepan.

Woks (3) and frying pans (4) also play a major role in one-pot cooking. Make sure you buy the right wok for your type of cooker; if you cook on electric rings, you'll need one with a flat base so that it comes into contact with the heat source.

It's a matter of personal preference whether you choose non-stick frying pans or not. They certainly make life easier for some recipes, such as egg-based dishes, as they're less likely to stick. However, it is harder to get good browning on foods as the non-stick pans cannot withstand a high heat.

The one thing that really is important is a good, thick base,

to allow the heat to spread evenly and maintain a constant temperature. If your new pan comes with instructions to season it before use, it is important to follow them, as seasoning helps to prolong the life of the pan.

Roasting Tins

Choose a roasting tin (5) in which the ingredients will fit comfortably, without over-crowding. If it's too full, they'll take longer to cook; if it's too empty, your ingredients may burn. Don't forget to check that the tin will fit inside your oven!

Chopping Boards

A good-quality, thick board will last for years. Remember to keep separate boards for raw and cooked meats and fish. (6)

Knives

Using the right-sized knife for the job is very important. There are two essential knives that should be in every kitchen. A chopping knife has a heavy, wide blade and comes in a variety of sizes. Choose one with a blade about 18–20 cm/7–8 in long; this makes it easy to handle and will be ideal for chopping vegetables, meats and herbs. (7) A paring knife has a small blade and is ideal for trimming and peeling all kinds of vegetables and fruits. (8)

Measuring Jugs and Spoons

Measure ingredients carefully when following a recipe. Good

measuring jugs (9) and spoons (10) make this far easier. Remember not to mix metric and imperial measurements.

Zester

A useful tool for cutting long, thin strips of orange, lemon or lime rind. Simply scrape over the surface – and there's no messy grater to wash up. The result is coarser than grated rind, but makes an attractive garnish. (11)

Pestle and Mortar

If you use fresh spices, a pestle and mortar is the perfect tool for crushing small amounts. (12)

Slotted Spoon

A simple utensil that is absolutely essential for one-pot cooking. When you lift browned meat from a pan, it allows the fat and juices to remain in the pan, so you don't lose valuable flavours. (13)

Browning Meat

This is very important when making stews and casseroles: the browner the meat, the richer the colour and flavour of the dish.

1 Heat the pan, with a little oil, until very hot. Don't add the meat when the fat is only warm or it won't seal the outside of the meat and you'll lose a lot of the meat juices.

2 Add a few pieces of meat at a time, depending on the size of the pan, and allow it to turn a rich golden brown, turning to brown all sides. Keep the heat quite high, but take care, as the fat will spit. Don't add the meat all at once as this reduces the heat dramatically and the meat will stew instead of sealing.

3 Remove the meat with a slotted spoon to drain off as much fat as possible, and place on kitchen paper. Repeat with the remaining meat.

Chopping an Onion

Chopped onions are used in many recipes and, whether they are finely or roughly chopped, the method is the same; just vary the gap between cuts to give different sized pieces.

1 Cut off the stalk end of the onion and cut it in half through the root, leaving the root intact. Remove the skin and place the halved onion, cut-side down, on the board. Make lengthways vertical cuts into the onion, taking care not to cut right through to the root.

2 Make two or three horizontal cuts from the stalk end through to the root, but without cutting all the way through.

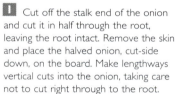

3 Cut the onion across from the stalk end to the root. The onion will fall away in small squares. Cut further apart for larger squares.

Using a Wok

Many one-pot recipes are suitable for cooking in a wok. It's a quick way to cook and, as long as the ingredients are prepared so they are similar in size, a good, evenly cooked result is achieved.

1 Make sure all the ingredients are prepared and close to hand before you start as wok cooking needs constant attention. Heat the wok for a few minutes before adding any oil.

2 When the pan is hot, add the oil and swirl it around to coat the base and sides of the wok. Allow the oil to heat for a few moments, then use a small piece of onion to test if the oil is sizzling hot.

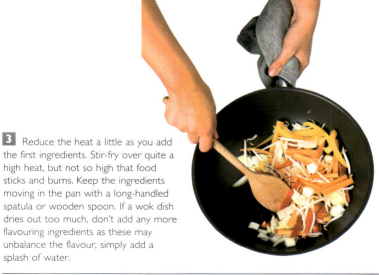

3 Reduce the heat a little as you add the first ingredients. Stir-fry over quite a high heat, but not so high that food sticks and burns. Keep the ingredients moving in the pan with a long-handled spatula or wooden spoon. If a wok dish dries out too much, don't add any more flavouring ingredients as these may unbalance the flavour, simply add a splash of water.

Peeling Tomatoes

If you have the time, peel tomatoes before adding them to sauces or stews. This avoids those unwanted, rolled-up, tough pieces of tomato skin!

1 Make a cross in each tomato with a sharp knife and place in a bowl.

2 Pour over enough boiling water to cover and leave to stand for 30 seconds. The skins should start to come away. Slightly unripe tomatoes may take a little longer.

3 Drain the tomatoes and peel the skin away with a sharp knife. Don't leave the tomatoes in the boiling water for too long as they tend to soften.

Preparing Fresh Ginger

Fresh root ginger can be used in slices, strips or finely chopped.

1 Peel the skin off the root with a peeler or a small, sharp knife. Then cut into thin strips, using a large, sharp knife.

2 Place each piece flat on the board, cut into fine strips and use, or turn the strips around and chop them finely.

Preparing Chillies

Chillies add a distinct flavour, but remove the seeds as they are fiery-hot.

1 Always protect your hands, as chillies can irritate the skin; wear rubber gloves and never rub your eyes after handling chillies. Halve the chilli lengthways and remove and discard the seeds.

2 Slice, finely chop and use as required. Wash the knife and board thoroughly in hot, soapy water. Always wash your hands thoroughly after preparing chillies.

Preparing Garlic

Don't worry if you don't have a garlic press: try this method, which gives wonderful juicy results.

1 Break off the clove of garlic, place the flat side of a large knife on top and strike with your fist. Remove all the papery outer skin. Begin by finely chopping the clove.

2 Sprinkle over a little table salt and, using the flat side of a large knife blade, work the salt into the garlic, until the clove softens and releases its juices. Use as required.

Preparing Lemon Grass

Use the whole stem and remove it before cooking, or chop the root.

1 Trim the end of the stem and trim off the tops, until you are left with about 10 cm/4 in.

2 Split in half lengthways and finely chop or, if the bulb is particularly fresh, thinly slice. Use as required.

Skinning Fish Fillets

It's easier to remove the skin before cooking than to flake the cooked fish away from it.

1 Lay the fish flat on a clean board, skin-side down, with the tail towards you. Using a sharp knife with a flexible blade, make a slit between the skin and flesh of the fillet.

2 Hold the skin with one hand. Place the knife between the skin and flesh with the edge against the skin and the blade almost parallel to it. Use a gentle sawing motion to remove the flesh, holding the skin taut underneath.

Chopping Herbs

Chop herbs just before you use them; the flavour will then be much better.

1 Remove the leaves and place on a clean dry board. Use a large, sharp cook's knife (a blunt knife will bruise, not chop, the herbs).

2 Chop the herbs, as finely or as coarsely as required, by holding the tip of the blade on the board and rocking the handle up and down.

Grating Citrus Rind

We've all spent ages trying to get citrus rind off a grater. Try a zester: it makes life much easier!

1 Hold the edge of the zester against the side of the fruit and pull towards you. The rind comes off easily, leaving the pith behind.

2 Continue around the fruit. If you prefer smaller pieces, simply chop the rind roughly.

Thinly Slicing Vegetables

Some of the recipes call for thinly sliced vegetables; without a food processor, this could be quite tricky, but not with this technique.

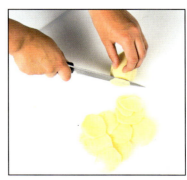

1 Peel the vegetables as required. Take a thin slice off one side, to give a solid base to stand on. This will prevent the vegetable from sliding around.

2 Stand the vegetable on its flat base and then thinly slice with a sharp knife. Keep your fingers tucked underneath, using your knuckles as a guide.

Beef Noodle Soup

A steaming bowl, packed with delicious flavours and a taste of the Orient.

Serves 4

INGREDIENTS

10 g/¹/₄ oz dried porcini mushrooms
6 spring onions
115 g/4 oz carrots
350 g/12 oz rump steak
about 30 ml/2 tbsp oil
1 garlic clove, crushed
2.5 cm/1 in piece fresh root ginger,
  peeled and finely chopped
1.2 litres/2 pints/5 cups beef stock
45 ml/3 tbsp light soy sauce
60 ml/4 tbsp dry sherry
75 g/3 oz thin egg noodles
75 g/3 oz spinach, shredded
salt and pepper

rump steak
egg noodles
oil
dry sherry
soy sauce
spring onions
beef stock
fresh root ginger
garlic
spinach
carrots
porcini mushrooms

1 Break the mushrooms into small pieces, place in a bowl and pour over 150 ml/¹/₄ pint/²/₃ cup of boiling water. Leave to soak for 15 minutes.

2 Shred the spring onions and carrots into 5 cm/2 in long, fine strips. Trim any fat off the meat and slice into thin strips.

3 Heat the oil in a large saucepan and cook the beef in batches until browned, adding a little more oil if necessary. Remove the beef with a slotted spoon and drain on kitchen paper.

4 Add the garlic, ginger, spring onions and carrots to the pan and stir-fry for 3 minutes.

5 Add the beef stock, the mushrooms and their soaking liquid, soy sauce, sherry and plenty of seasoning. Bring to the boil and simmer, covered, for 10 minutes.

6 Break up the noodles slightly and add to the pan, with the spinach. Simmer gently for 5 minutes, or until the beef is tender. Adjust the seasoning before serving.

Thai-style Chicken Soup

A fragrant blend of coconut milk, lemon grass, ginger and lime makes a delicious soup, with just a hint of chilli.

Serves 4

INGREDIENTS
5 ml/1 tsp oil
1–2 fresh red chillies, seeded
   and chopped
2 garlic cloves, crushed
1 large leek, thinly sliced
600 ml/1 pint/2½ cups chicken
   stock
400 ml/14 fl oz/1⅔ cups
   coconut milk
450 g/1 lb boneless, skinless chicken
   thighs, cut into bite-sized pieces
30 ml/2 tbsp Thai fish sauce
1 lemon grass stick, split
2.5 cm/1 in piece fresh root ginger,
   peeled and finely chopped
5 ml/1 tsp sugar
4 kaffir lime leaves (optional)
75 g/3 oz/¾ cup frozen peas, thawed
45 ml/3 tbsp chopped
   fresh coriander

peas   *chicken stock*

oil   *chicken thighs*

sugar

fresh coriander   *red chillies*

fresh root ginger   *garlic*   *Thai fish sauce*   *coconut milk*   *lemon grass*   *leek*   *kaffir lime leaves*

1 Heat the oil in a large saucepan and cook the chillies and garlic for about 2 minutes. Add the leek and cook for a further 2 minutes.

2 Stir in the stock and coconut milk and bring to the boil.

3 Add the chicken, with the fish sauce, lemon grass, ginger, sugar and lime leaves, if using. Simmer, covered, for 15 minutes, or until the chicken is tender, stirring occasionally.

4 Add the peas and cook for a further 3 minutes. Remove the lemon grass and stir in the coriander just before serving.

Curried Salmon Chowder

A hint of mild curry paste really enhances the flavour of this soup, without making it too spicy.

Serves 4

INGREDIENTS

50 g/2 oz/4 tbsp butter
225 g/8 oz onions, roughly chopped
10 ml/2 tsp mild curry paste
150 ml/¼ pint/⅔ cup white wine
300 ml/½ pint/1¼ cups
    double cream
50 g/2 oz creamed coconut, grated
350 g/12 oz potatoes, peeled and
    finely chopped
450 g/1 lb salmon fillet, skinned and
    cut into bite-sized pieces
60 ml/4 tbsp chopped fresh flat
    leaf parsley
salt and pepper

onions

butter

salmon fillet

potatoes

white wine

double cream

curry paste

creamed coconut

flat leaf parsley

1 Melt the butter in a large saucepan, add the onions and cook over a low heat for 3–4 minutes, or until beginning to soften. Add the curry paste and cook for 1 minute more.

2 Add 475 ml/16 fl oz/2 cups water, the wine, cream, creamed coconut and a little seasoning. Bring to the boil, stirring until the coconut has dissolved smoothly.

3 Add the potatoes and simmer, covered, for about 15 minutes, or until they are almost tender.

4 Gently stir in the fish, taking care not to break it up too much. Simmer over a very low heat for 2–3 minutes, or until just tender. Add the parsley and adjust the seasoning. Serve immediately.

Mediterranean Fish Soup

This is delicious served with a rich garlic mayonnaise and plenty of crusty bread to mop up the juices. Use as many varieties of fish and shellfish as you can find.

Serves 4

INGREDIENTS

450 g/1 lb mixed fish fillets, such as red mullet, monkfish, sea bass and/or mackerel
450 g/1 lb mixed uncooked shellfish, such as mussels and prawns
pinch of saffron strands
60 ml/4 tbsp olive oil
350 g/12 oz onions, roughly chopped
350 g/12 oz fennel, halved and thinly sliced (about 1 small bulb)
10 ml/2 tsp plain flour
400 g/14 oz can chopped tomatoes, strained
3 garlic cloves, crushed
2 bay leaves
30 ml/2 tbsp chopped fresh thyme
pared rind of 1 orange
salt and cayenne pepper
garlic mayonnaise and crusty bread, to serve

1 Wash and skin the fish, if necessary, and cut into large chunks. Clean the shellfish and remove the heads from the prawns.

mixed fish fillets

chopped tomatoes

plain flour

bay leaves
orange
garlic
olive oil
prawns
onions

cayenne pepper

fennel
mussels
garlic mayonnaise

thyme
saffron

2 Place the saffron strands in a bowl and pour over 150 ml/¼ pint/⅔ cup boiling water. Leave the saffron to soak for about 20 minutes. Strain.

3 Heat the oil in a large saucepan and add the onions and fennel. Fry gently for 5 minutes, stirring occasionally, or until beginning to soften.

4 Stir in the flour. Gradually blend in 750 ml/1¼ pints/3 cups water, the tomatoes, garlic, bay leaves, thyme, orange rind, saffron liquid and seasoning to taste. Bring to the boil.

5 Reduce the heat and add the fish (not the shellfish) and simmer very gently, uncovered, for about 2 minutes.

6 Add the shellfish and cook for a further 2–3 minutes, or until all the fish is cooked but still holding its shape. Discard any mussels that haven't opened. Adjust the seasoning. Serve in warmed bowls, with a generous spoonful of garlic mayonnaise and plenty of crusty bread.

Squash, Bacon and Swiss Cheese Soup

A lightly spiced squash soup, enriched with plenty of creamy melting cheese.

Serves 4

INGREDIENTS

900 g/2 lb butternut squash
  or pumpkin
225 g/8 oz smoked back bacon
15 ml/1 tbsp oil
225 g/8 oz onions, roughly chopped
2 garlic cloves, crushed
10 ml/2 tsp ground cumin
15 ml/1 tbsp ground coriander
275 g/10 oz potatoes, peeled and cut
  into small chunks
900 ml/1½ pints/3¾ cups
  vegetable stock
10 ml/2 tsp cornflour
30 ml/2 tbsp crème fraîche
Tabasco sauce, to taste
175 g/6 oz/1½ cups Gruyère
  cheese, grated
salt and pepper

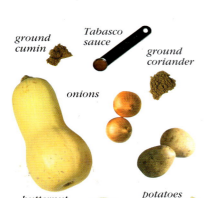

ground cumin

Tabasco sauce

ground coriander

onions

butternut squash

potatoes

garlic

oil

Gruyère cheese

cornflour

bacon

crème fraîche

vegetable stock

1 Cut the squash or pumpkin into large pieces. Using a sharp knife, carefully remove the skin, wasting as little as possible.

2 Scoop out the seeds and chop the squash or pumpkin into small chunks. Remove all the fat from the bacon and roughly chop the meat.

3 Heat the oil in a large saucepan and cook the onions and garlic for 3 minutes, or until beginning to soften.

4 Add the bacon and cook for about 3 minutes. Stir in the spices and cook for a further 1 minute.

5 Add the chopped squash or pumpkin, potatoes and stock. Bring to the boil and simmer for 15 minutes, or until the squash or pumpkin and potatoes are tender.

6 Blend the cornflour with 30 ml/ 2 tbsp water and add to the soup, with the crème fraîche. Bring to the boil and simmer, uncovered, for 3 minutes. Adjust the seasoning and add Tabasco sauce to taste. Ladle the soup into warm bowls and sprinkle over the cheese; it will just begin to melt. Serve immediately.

Caramelized Onion Soup

The onions are cooked very slowly to give this soup its rich, brown colour and delicious sweet onion flavour.

Serves 4

INGREDIENTS
30 ml/2 tbsp olive oil
25 g/1 oz/2 tbsp butter
900 g/2 lb onions, quartered
    and sliced
2 garlic cloves, crushed
5 ml/1 tsp caraway seeds
15 ml/1 tbsp soft light brown sugar
15 ml/1 tbsp balsamic vinegar
10 ml/2 tsp plain flour
1.2 litres/2 pints/5 cups
    vegetable stock
1.5 ml/¼ tsp yeast extract
grated rind and juice of 1 lemon
salt and pepper
sliced French bread and grated
    Emmenthal cheese, to serve

caraway seeds

butter

Emmenthal cheese

French bread

onions

lemon

garlic

olive oil

soft light brown sugar

plain flour

yeast extract

balsamic vinegar

vegetable stock

1 Heat the oil and butter in a large saucepan and add the onions, garlic, caraway seeds and sugar. Cook, covered, over a medium heat, for about 20 minutes, stirring occasionally.

2 Add the balsamic vinegar and cook, uncovered, for a further 10 minutes until softened and well browned. Stir in the flour and cook over a low heat for 1 minute.

3 Turn off the heat and gradually blend in the stock and yeast extract and season well. Bring to the boil, stirring, and simmer, uncovered, for about 5 minutes.

4 Stir in the grated lemon rind and 15 ml/1 tbsp of the juice and adjust the seasoning. Serve the soup topped with slices of French bread and grated Emmenthal cheese.

Spicy Peanut Soup

A thick and warming vegetable soup, flavoured with chilli and peanuts.

Serves 6

INGREDIENTS

30 ml/2 tbsp oil
1 large onion, finely chopped
2 garlic cloves, crushed
5 ml/1 tsp mild chilli powder
2 red peppers, seeded and
　finely chopped
225 g/8 oz carrots, finely chopped
225 g/8 oz potatoes, peeled and
　finely chopped
3 celery sticks, sliced
900 ml/1½ pints/3¾ cups
　vegetable stock
90 ml/6 tbsp crunchy peanut butter
115 g/4 oz/⅔ cup sweetcorn
salt and pepper
roughly chopped unsalted roasted
　peanuts, to garnish

mild chilli powder

carrots

onion

sweetcorn

celery

garlic

peanut butter

oil

red peppers

potatoes

vegetable stock

roasted peanuts

1 Heat the oil in a large pan and cook the onion and garlic for about 3 minutes. Add the chilli powder and cook for a further 1 minute.

2 Add the peppers, carrots, potatoes and celery. Stir well, then cook for a further 4 minutes, stirring occasionally.

3 Stir in the stock, peanut butter and sweetcorn until combined.

4 Season well. Bring to the boil, cover and simmer for about 20 minutes, or until all the vegetables are tender. Adjust the seasoning before serving, sprinkled with the chopped peanuts.

Fresh Tomato and Bean Soup

A rich chunky tomato soup, with beans and coriander. Serve with olive ciabatta.

Serves 4

INGREDIENTS
900 g/2 lb ripe plum tomatoes
30 ml/2 tbsp olive oil
275 g/10 oz onions, roughly chopped
2 garlic cloves, crushed
900 ml/1½ pints/3¾ cups
   vegetable stock
30 ml/2 tbsp sun-dried tomato paste
10 ml/2 tsp paprika
15 ml/1 tbsp cornflour
425 g/15 oz can cannellini beans,
   rinsed and drained
30 ml/2 tbsp chopped fresh coriander
salt and pepper
olive ciabatta, to serve

sun-dried tomato paste

cannellini beans

olive oil

fresh coriander

garlic

plum tomatoes

cornflour

paprika

vegetable stock

onions

1 First, peel the tomatoes. Using a sharp knife, make a small cross in each one and place in a bowl. Pour over boiling water to cover and leave to stand for 30–60 seconds.

2 Drain the tomatoes and peel off the skins. Quarter them and then cut each piece in half again.

3 Heat the oil in a large saucepan and cook the onions and garlic for 3 minutes, or until just beginning to soften.

4 Add the tomatoes to the onions, with the stock, sun-dried tomato paste and paprika. Season with a little salt and pepper. Bring to the boil and simmer for 10 minutes.

5 Mix the cornflour to a paste with 30 ml/2 tbsp water. Stir the beans into the soup with the cornflour paste. Cook for a further 5 minutes.

6 Adjust the seasoning and stir in the chopped coriander just before you serve with olive ciabatta.

Gazpacho

A traditional, chilled Spanish soup, perfect for a summer lunch. Make sure all the ingredients are in peak condition for the best flavoured soup.

Serves 6

INGREDIENTS

1 green pepper, seeded and
  roughly chopped
1 red pepper, seeded and
  roughly chopped
½ cucumber, roughly chopped
1 onion, roughly chopped
1 fresh red chilli, seeded and
  roughly chopped
450 g/1 lb ripe plum tomatoes,
  roughly chopped
900 ml/1½ pints/3¾ cups passata or
  tomato juice
30 ml/2 tbsp red wine vinegar
30 ml/2 tbsp olive oil
15 ml/1 tbsp caster sugar
salt and pepper
crushed ice, to garnish (optional)

olive oil

passata

red wine vinegar

green pepper

caster sugar

plum tomatoes

red pepper

red chilli

onion

cucumber

1 Reserve a small piece of green and red pepper, cucumber and onion: finely chop, and set aside as a garnish.

2 Process all the remaining ingredients (except the ice) in a blender or food processor until smooth. You may need to do this in batches.

3 Pass the soup through a sieve into a clean glass bowl, pushing it through with a spoon to extract as much flavour as possible.

4 Adjust the seasoning and chill. Serve sprinkled with the reserved chopped peppers, cucumber and onion. For an extra special touch, add a little crushed ice to the garnish.

Garlic, Chick-pea and Spinach Soup

This delicious, thick and creamy soup is richly flavoured and perfect for vegetarians.

Serves 4

INGREDIENTS

30 ml/2 tbsp olive oil
4 garlic cloves, crushed
1 onion, roughly chopped
10 ml/2 tsp ground cumin
10 ml/2 tsp ground coriander
1.2 litres/2 pints/5 cups
    vegetable stock
350 g/12 oz potatoes, peeled and
    finely chopped
425 g/15 oz can chick-peas, drained
15 ml/1 tbsp cornflour
150 ml/¼ pint/⅔ cup double cream
30 ml/2 tbsp light tahini (sesame
    seed paste)
200 g/7 oz spinach, shredded
cayenne pepper
salt and pepper

light tahini   cornflour

chick-peas   cayenne   ground
              pepper   coriander

double
cream   garlic   spinach

onion   potatoes   vegetable   ground   olive
                     stock   cumin   oil

1 Heat the oil in a large saucepan and cook the garlic and onion for 5 minutes, or until they are softened and golden brown.

2 Stir in the cumin and coriander and cook for a further minute.

3 Pour in the stock and add the potatoes. Bring to the boil and simmer for 10 minutes. Add the drained chick-peas and simmer for a further 5 minutes, or until the potatoes and chick-peas are just tender.

4 Blend together the cornflour, cream, tahini and plenty of seasoning. Stir into the soup with the spinach. Bring to the boil, stirring, and simmer for a further 2 minutes. Adjust the seasoning with salt, pepper and cayenne pepper to taste. Serve immediately, sprinkled with a little cayenne pepper.

Cassoulet

Based on the traditional French dish, this recipe is full of delicious flavours and makes a welcoming and warming meal.

Serves 6

INGREDIENTS

450 g/1 lb boneless duck breast
225 g/8 oz thick-cut streaky pork or
    unsmoked streaky bacon rashers
450 g/1 lb Toulouse or
    garlic sausages
45 ml/3 tbsp oil
450 g/1 lb onions, chopped
2 garlic cloves, crushed
2 x 425 g/15 oz cans cannellini
    beans, rinsed and drained
225 g/8 oz carrots, roughly chopped
400 g/14 oz can chopped tomatoes
15 ml/1 tbsp tomato purée
1 bouquet garni
30 ml/2 tbsp chopped fresh thyme
475 ml/16 fl oz/2 cups chicken stock
115 g/4 oz/2 cups fresh breadcrumbs
salt and pepper
fresh thyme sprigs, to
    garnish (optional)
salad leaves, to serve

garlic

garlic
sausages

chicken
stock

streaky
pork

fresh
breadcrumbs

cannellini
beans

tomato
purée

fresh
thyme

chopped
tomatoes

oil

duck breast

bouquet
garni

carrots

onions

1 Preheat the oven to 160°C/325°F/Gas 3. Cut the duck breast and pork or bacon rashers into large pieces. Twist the sausages and cut into short lengths.

2 Heat the oil in a large flameproof casserole. Cook the meat in batches, until well browned. Remove from the pan with a slotted spoon and drain on kitchen paper.

3 Add the onions and garlic to the pan and cook for 3–4 minutes, or until beginning to soften, stirring frequently.

4 Stir in the beans, carrots, tomatoes, tomato purée, bouquet garni, thyme and seasoning. Return the meat to the pan and mix until well combined.

5 Add enough of the stock just to cover the meat and beans. (The cassoulet shouldn't be swimming in juices; if the mixture becomes too dry add a little more stock or water.) Bring to the boil. Cover tightly and cook in the oven for 1 hour.

6 Remove the cassoulet from the oven, add a little more stock or water, if necessary, and remove the bouquet garni. Sprinkle over the breadcrumbs and return to the oven, uncovered, for a further 40 minutes, or until the meat is tender and the top crisp. Brown under the grill, if necessary, and garnish with fresh thyme sprigs (if using). Serve with plenty of salad.

Chicken Casserole

A casserole of wonderfully tender chicken, root vegetables and lentils, finished with crème fraîche, mustard and tarragon.

Serves 4

INGREDIENTS

350 g/12 oz onions
350 g/12 oz trimmed leeks
225 g/8 oz carrots
450 g/1 lb swede
30 ml/2 tbsp oil
4 chicken portions, about 900 g/2 lb
    total weight
115 g/4 oz/½ cup green lentils
475 ml/16 fl oz/2 cups chicken stock
300 ml/½ pint/1¼ cups apple juice
10 ml/2 tsp cornflour
45 ml/3 tbsp crème fraîche
10 ml/2 tsp wholegrain mustard
30 ml/2 tbsp chopped fresh tarragon
salt and pepper
fresh tarragon sprigs, to garnish

fresh tarragon

crème fraîche

oil

leeks

onions

swede

carrots

chicken portions

apple juice

wholegrain mustard

chicken stock

green lentils

cornflour

1 Preheat the oven to 190°C/375°F/Gas 5. Prepare the onions, leeks, carrots and swede and roughly chop into similarly sized pieces.

2 Heat the oil in a large flameproof casserole. Season the chicken portions with salt and pepper and brown them in the hot oil until golden. Drain on kitchen paper.

3 Add the onions to the pan and cook for 5 minutes, stirring, until they begin to soften and colour.

4 Stir in the leeks, carrots, swede and lentils and stir over a medium heat for 2 minutes.

5 Return the chicken to the pan. Add the stock, apple juice and seasoning. Bring to the boil and cover tightly. Cook in the oven for 50–60 minutes, or until the chicken and lentils are tender.

6 Place the casserole on the hob over a medium heat. Blend the cornflour with 30 ml/2 tbsp water and add to the casserole with the crème fraîche, mustard and tarragon. Adjust the seasoning. Simmer gently for about 2 minutes, stirring, before serving, garnished with tarragon sprigs.

Citrus Beef Curry

This superbly aromatic Thai-style curry is not too hot but full of flavour. For a special meal, it goes perfectly with Thai Fried Noodles.

Serves 4

INGREDIENTS

450 g/1 lb rump steak
30 ml/2 tbsp oil
30 ml/2 tbsp medium curry paste
2 bay leaves
400 ml/14 fl oz/1²/₃ cups
    coconut milk
300 ml/¹/₂ pint/1¹/₄ cups beef stock
30 ml/2 tbsp lemon juice
45 ml/3 tbsp Thai fish sauce
15 ml/1 tbsp caster sugar
115 g/4 oz baby onions, peeled but
    left whole
225 g/8oz new potatoes, halved
115g/4 oz/²/₃ cup unsalted roasted
    peanuts, roughly chopped
115 g/4 oz fine green beans, halved
1 red pepper, seeded and
    thinly sliced
unsalted roasted peanuts,
    to garnish (optional)

rump steak

peanuts

curry paste

red pepper

baby onions

bay leaves

fine green beans

new potatoes

oil

lemon juice

Thai fish sauce

caster sugar

coconut milk

beef stock

1 Trim any fat off the beef and cut into strips about 5 cm/2 in long.

2 Heat the oil in a saucepan and cook the curry paste over a medium heat for 30 seconds.

3 Stir in the beef and cook for 2 minutes until it's beginning to brown and is coated with the spices.

4 Stir in the bay leaves, coconut milk, stock, lemon juice, fish sauce and sugar. Bring to the boil, stirring.

5 Add the onions and potatoes, then bring back to the boil, reduce the heat and leave to simmer, uncovered, for 5 minutes.

6 Stir in the peanuts, beans and pepper and simmer for a further 10 minutes, or until the beef and potatoes are tender. Cook for a little longer, if necessary. Serve in shallow bowls, with a spoon and fork, to enjoy all the rich and creamy juices. Sprinkle with extra unsalted roasted peanuts, if you wish.

Zesty Lamb Stew

Succulent lamb in a warming spiced gravy, with a refreshing hint of orange, is perfect served alone or with a fresh green vegetable.

Serves 6

INGREDIENTS
1.4 kg/3 lb leg of lamb, boned or
    900 g/2 lb boneless leg of lamb
30 ml/2 tbsp plain flour
about 45 ml/3 tbsp oil
275 g/10 oz onions, roughly chopped
2 garlic cloves, crushed
2 cinnamon sticks
2 red peppers, seeded and
    roughly chopped
15 ml/1 tbsp ground ginger
65 g/2½ oz/⅓ cup pearl barley
900 ml/1½ pints/3¾ cups lamb or
    beef stock
30 ml/2 tbsp Worcestershire sauce
grated rind and juice of 1 orange
450 g/1 lb potatoes, roughly
    chopped
500 g/1¼ lb swede, peeled and
    roughly chopped
salt and pepper

1 Preheat the oven to 180°C/350°F/ Gas 4. Trim any fat off the meat and cut into large cubes. Season the flour and toss the lamb in it to coat the pieces.

2 Heat the oil in a large flameproof casserole and brown the meat in batches, adding a little more oil if necessary. Remove with a slotted spoon and drain on kitchen paper.

3 Add the onions and garlic to the pan and cook for 3–4 minutes until they are beginning to soften and colour, stirring frequently.

oil

ground ginger

swede

cinnamon sticks

garlic

leg of lamb

Worcestershire sauce

potatoes

onions

lamb or beef stock

pearl barley

plain flour

orange

red peppers

4 Stir in the cinnamon sticks, red peppers, ginger and pearl barley. Cook over a medium heat for a further 2 minutes. Add any remaining flour to the pan and cook for 1 minute.

5 Blend in the stock with the Worcestershire sauce, grated rind of the orange and 45 ml/3 tbsp of the juice. Season well and bring to the boil.

6 Return the meat to the pan with the potatoes and swede. Cover tightly and cook in the oven for about 1 hour 20 minutes, or until the meat and vegetables are tender. Adjust the seasoning before serving.

Fruity Cider Pork with Parsley Dumplings

Pork and fruit are a perfect combination. If you don't want to make dumplings, serve creamy mashed potatoes with the stew.

Serves 6

INGREDIENTS

115 g/4 oz/scant ¹/₂ cup pitted prunes, roughly chopped
115 g/4 oz/scant ¹/₄ cup dried apricots, roughly chopped
300 ml/¹/₂ pint/1¹/₄ cups dry cider
30 ml/2 tbsp plain flour
675 g/1¹/₂ lb lean boneless pork, cut into cubes
30 ml/2 tbsp oil
350 g/12 oz onions, roughly chopped
2 garlic cloves, crushed
6 celery sticks, roughly chopped
475 ml/16 fl oz/2 cups stock
12 juniper berries, lightly crushed
30 ml/2 tbsp chopped fresh thyme
115 g/4 oz self-raising flour
50 g/2 oz/generous ¹/₃ cup vegetable suet
45 ml/3 tbsp chopped fresh parsley
425 g/15 oz can black-eyed beans, drained
salt and pepper

1 Preheat the oven to 180°C/350°F/ Gas 4. Place the prunes and apricots in a small bowl. Pour over the cider and leave to soak for at least 20 minutes.

2 Season the flour. Toss the pork in the flour to coat; reserve any leftover flour. Heat the oil in a large flameproof casserole. Brown the meat in batches, adding a little more oil if necessary. Remove with a slotted spoon and drain on kitchen paper.

fresh parsley

celery

plain flour

fresh thyme

onions

vegetable suet

garlic

dried apricots

pork

prunes

dry cider

juniper berries

black-eyed beans

oil

self-raising flour

stock

3 Add the onions, garlic and celery to the casserole and cook for 5 minutes. Add any remaining flour and cook for a further 1 minute.

4 Blend in the stock until smooth. Add the cider and fruit, juniper berries, thyme and plenty of seasoning. Bring to the boil, add the pork, cover tightly and cook in the oven for 50 minutes.

5 Just before the end of cooking time prepare the dumplings. Sift the flour into a bowl, then stir in the suet and parsley. Add about 90 ml/6 tbsp water and mix together to give a smooth dough

6 Remove the casserole from the oven, stir in the beans and adjust the seasoning. Divide the dumpling mixture into six, form into rounds and place on top. Return to the oven, covered, and cook for a further 20–25 minutes, or until the dumplings are cooked and the pork is tender.

Fish Casserole with Lemon Grass

Lemon grass gives this delicate fish casserole an aromatic flavour, perfect for a special treat.

Serves 4

INGREDIENTS
25 g/1 oz/2 tbsp butter
175 g/6 oz onions, chopped
20 ml/4 tsp plain flour
400 ml/14 fl oz/1²/₃ cups stock
150 ml/¹/₄ pint/²/₃ cup white wine
2.5 cm/1 in piece fresh root ginger, peeled and finely chopped
2 lemon grass stalks, trimmed and finely chopped
450 g/1 lb new potatoes, scrubbed and halved if necessary
450 g/1 lb white fish fillets, skinned
175 g/6 oz large peeled cooked prawns
275 g/10 oz small broccoli florets
150 ml/¹/₄ pint/²/₃ cup double cream
60 ml/4 tbsp chopped fresh garlic chives
salt and pepper
crusty bread, to serve

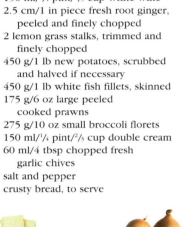

butter

onions

white wine

white fish fillets

prawns

broccoli *lemon grass* *double cream* *fresh root ginger* *plain flour* *garlic chives* *new potatoes* *stock*

1 Melt the butter in a large saucepan. Cook the onions for 3–4 minutes, or until just tender. Stir in the flour and cook for 1 minute.

2 Stir in the stock, wine, ginger, lemon grass and potatoes. Season well and bring to the boil. Cover and cook for 15 minutes, or until the potatoes are almost tender.

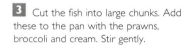

3 Cut the fish into large chunks. Add these to the pan with the prawns, broccoli and cream. Stir gently.

4 Simmer gently for 5 minutes, taking care not to break up the fish. Adjust the seasoning and stir in the chives. Serve with plenty of crusty bread.

Pot-roast Chicken with Lemon and Garlic

This is a rustic dish that is easy to prepare. Lardons are thick strips of bacon fat; if you can't get them, use streaky bacon.

Serves 4

INGREDIENTS
30 ml/2 tbsp olive oil
25 g/1 oz/2 tbsp butter
175 g/6 oz/1 cup smoked lardons or
    streaky bacon, roughly chopped
8 whole garlic cloves, peeled
4 onions, quartered
10 ml/2 tsp plain flour
600 ml/1 pint/2½ cups chicken stock
2 lemons, thickly sliced
45 ml/3 tbsp chopped fresh thyme
1 oven-ready chicken, about
    1.5 kg/3–3½ lb
2 x 400 g/14 oz cans flageolet beans,
    drained and rinsed
salt and pepper
bread, to serve

smoked lardons
lemons
chicken
butter
garlic
flageolet beans
onions
thyme
olive oil
plain flour
chicken stock

1 Preheat the oven to 190°C/375°F/ Gas 5. Heat the oil and butter in a flameproof casserole that is large enough to hold the chicken w th a little extra room around the sides. Add the lardons or bacon and cook until golden. Remove with a slotted spoon and drain on kitchen paper.

2 Brown the garlic and onions over a high heat until the edges are caramelized. Stir in the flour, then the stock. Return the bacon to the pan with the lemon, thyme and seasoning.

3 Bring to the boil, then place the chicken on top, season and transfer to the oven. Cook for 1 hour, basting the chicken occasionally.

4 Baste the chicken with the juices. Stir the beans into the pan and return to the oven for a further 30 minutes, or until the chicken is cooked through and tender. Carve the chicken into thick slices and serve with the beans and plenty of bread, to mop up the juices.

Pot-roast Beef with Guinness

This heart-warming, rich pot-roast is ideal for a winter's supper. Brisket of beef has the best flavour but this dish works equally well with rolled silverside or topside.

Serves 6

INGREDIENTS
30 ml/2 tbsp oil
900 g/2 lb rolled brisket of beef
275 g/10 oz onions, roughly chopped
6 celery sticks, thickly sliced
450 g/1 lb carrots, cut into
    large chunks
675 g/1½ lb potatoes, cut into
    large chunks
30 ml/2 tbsp plain flour
475 ml/16 fl oz/2 cups beef stock
300 ml/½ pint/1¼ cups Guinness
1 bay leaf
45 ml/3 tbsp chopped fresh thyme
5 ml/1 tsp soft brown sugar
30 ml/2 tbsp wholegrain mustard
15 ml/1 tbsp tomato purée
salt and pepper

potatoes

thyme

plain flour

beef stock

bay leaf

rolled brisket of beef

oil

Guinness

wholegrain mustard

onions

celery

carrots

tomato purée

soft brown sugar

1 Preheat the oven to 180°C/350°F/ Gas 4. Heat the oil in a large flameproof casserole and brown the meat all over until golden. Remove from the pan and drain on kitchen paper.

2 Add the onions and cook for 4 minutes, or until beginning to soften and turn brown, stirring all the time.

3 Add the celery, carrots and potatoes and cook over a medium heat for 2–3 minutes, or until they are beginning to colour.

4 Add the flour and cook for a further 1 minute. Blend in the stock and Guinness until combined. Bring to the boil, stirring.

5 Stir in the bay leaf, thyme, sugar, mustard, tomato purée and plenty of seasoning. Place the meat on top, cover tightly and transfer to the oven.

6 Cook for about 2½ hours, or until the vegetables and meat are tender. Adjust the seasoning and add another pinch of sugar, if necessary. To serve, remove the meat and carve into thick slices. Serve with the vegetables and plenty of Guinness gravy.

Pot-roast Glazed Lamb

The vegetables in this pot-roast turn tender and caramelized, with all the wonderful flavours of the meat. Spoon the juices over during cooking.

Serves 6

INGREDIENTS

12 garlic cloves
1.1 kg/2½ lb leg of lamb
 (knuckle end)
about 12 small fresh rosemary sprigs
45 ml/3 tbsp olive oil
12 shallots, peeled
900 g/2 lb potatoes, cut into chunks
675 g/1½ lb parsnips, cut into
 large chunks
675 g/1½ lb/ carrots, cut into chunks
300 ml/½ pint/1¼ cups red wine
45 ml/3 tbsp clear honey
30 ml/2 tbsp dark soy sauce
10 ml/2 tsp plain flour
475 ml/16 fl oz/2 cups lamb stock
salt and pepper
fresh rosemary sprigs, to garnish

dark soy sauce

leg of lamb

olive oil

rosemary

honey

carrots

potatoes

parsnips

garlic

shallots

red wine   plain flour   lamb stock

1 Preheat the oven to 190°C/375°F/ Gas 5. Peel three of the cloves of garlic and slice. Make slits all over the meat and insert slices of garlic and small sprigs of rosemary. Season well.

2 Heat the oil in a large flameproof casserole or roasting tin and add the shallots. Cook, stirring occasionally, until they begin to turn golden.

3 Add the potatoes, parsnips, carrots and remaining unpeeled cloves of garlic. Stir to coat in the oil. Season. Place the lamb on top and pour over half the red wine. Cover tightly, place in the oven and cook for 1 hour; baste occasionally with any fat and juices.

4 Mix together the honey and soy sauce until combined. After the first hour of cooking, pour the honey mixture over the lamb and baste. Return to the oven, uncovered, for a further 1–1¼ hours, basting the meat and vegetables from time to time.

5 Test that the meat is cooked and the vegetables are tender. Remove from the pan and leave the meat to rest for 10–15 minutes before carving (keep the vegetables warm).

6 Place the ccasserole or roasting tin on the hob, stir in the flour and cook for 1 minute. Blend in the stock and remaining wine, then bring to the boil and adjust the seasoning. Serve the meat and vegetables with plenty of the sauce spooned over them, garnished with rosemary.

Mediterranean Chicken

This is the perfect after-work supper-party dish: it is quick to prepare and full of sunshine flavours.

Serves 4

INGREDIENTS

4 chicken breast portions, about
    675 g/1½ lb total weight
115 g/4 oz/1 cup soft cheese with
    garlic and herbs
450 g/1 lb courgettes
2 red peppers, seeded
450 g/1 lb plum tomatoes
4 celery sticks
about 30 ml/2 tbsp olive oil
275 g/10 oz onions, roughly chopped
3 garlic cloves, crushed
8 sun-dried tomatoes,
    roughly chopped
5 ml/1 tsp dried oregano
30 ml/2 tbsp balsamic vinegar
5 ml/1 tsp paprika
salt and pepper
olive ciabatta or crusty bread,
    to serve

1 Preheat the oven to 190°C/375°F/ Gas 5. Loosen the skin of each chicken portion, without removing it, to make a pocket. Divide the cheese into four and push one quarter underneath the skin of each chicken portion in an even layer.

2 Cut the courgettes and peppers into similarly sized chunky pieces. Quarter the tomatoes and slice the celery sticks.

3 Heat 30 ml/2 tbsp of the oil in a large, shallow flameproof casserole. Cook the onions and garlic for 4 minutes until they are soft and golden, stirring frequently.

4 Add the courgettes, peppers and celery and cook for a further 5 minutes.

5 Stir in the tomatoes, sun-dried tomatoes, oregano and balsamic vinegar. Season well.

6 Place the chicken on top, drizzle over a little more olive oil and season with salt and the paprika. Bake in the oven for 35–40 minutes or until the chicken is golden and cooked through. Serve with plenty of olive ciabatta or crusty bread.

olive oil

paprika

celery

chicken

sun-dried tomatoes

dried oregano

garlic

onions

courgettes

soft cheese with garlic and herbs

red peppers

balsamic vinegar

plum tomatoes

Summer Tomato Pasta

This is a deliciously light pasta dish, full of fresh flavours. Use buffalo-milk mozzarella, if you can: its flavour is noticeably better.

Serves 4

INGREDIENTS
275 g/10 oz/2¼ cups dried penne
450 g/1 lb plum tomatoes
275 g/10 oz mozzarella, drained
60 ml/4 tbsp olive oil
15 ml/1 tbsp balsamic vinegar
grated rind and juice of 1 lemon
15 fresh basil leaves, shredded
salt and black pepper
fresh basil leaves, to garnish

balsamic vinegar

basil

lemon   mozzarella

plum tomatoes   penne

olive oil

1 Cook the pasta in boiling, salted water according to packet instructions, until just tender.

2 Quarter the tomatoes and remove the seeds, then chop the flesh into cubes. Cut the mozzarella into similarly sized pieces.

3 Mix together the olive oil, balsamic vinegar, grated lemon rind, 15 ml/1 tbsp of the lemon juice and the basil. Season. Add the tomatoes and mozzarella and leave to stand until the pasta is cooked.

4 Drain the pasta and toss with the tomato mixture. Serve immediately, garnished with fresh basil leaves.

Garlic and Herb Pasta

A tasty pasta dish served with plenty of fresh Parmesan cheese, this recipe makes a speedy and satisfying supper.

Serves 4

INGREDIENTS

250 g/9 oz mixed egg and
  spinach tagliatelle
3 garlic cloves, crushed
2 canned anchovy fillets, drained
  and rinsed
30 ml/2 tbsp drained capers,
  finely chopped
5 ml/1 tsp Dijon mustard
50 ml/2 fl oz/¼ cup olive oil
60 ml/4 tbsp mixed chopped fresh
  chives, parsley and oregano
50 g/2 oz/⅓ cup pine nuts, toasted
15 ml/1 tbsp lemon juice
salt and pepper
freshly shaved Parmesan cheese,
  to serve

oregano

capers

chives

anchovy
fillets

olive
oil

pine nuts

Dijon mustard

tagliatelle

garlic

parsley

lemon juice

Parmesan cheese

1 Cook the pasta in boiling, salted water, according to the packet instructions, until just tender.

2 Using a pestle and mortar, pound the garlic and anchovy until combined. Transfer to a bowl, add the capers and mustard and mix well.

3 Gradually drizzle in the olive oil, mixing until thoroughly combined. Stir in the herbs, pine nuts and lemon juice. Season well.

4 Drain the pasta and toss together with the herb dressing, until well combined. Serve, sprinkled with plenty of shaved Parmesan cheese.

Jambalaya

This Cajun dish comes from the deep south of the USA. It contains a wonderful combination of rice, meat and fish, with a kick of chilli. If you like *really* spicy food, add a little more chilli powder.

Serves 6

INGREDIENTS
450 g/1 lb boneless, skinless
   chicken thighs
225 g/8 oz chorizo or spicy sausages
5 celery sticks
1 red pepper, seeded
1 green pepper, seeded
about 30 ml/2 tbsp oil
225 g/8 oz onions, roughly chopped
2 garlic cloves, crushed
10 ml/2 tsp mild chilli powder
2.5 ml/$\frac{1}{2}$ tsp ground ginger
300 g/11 oz/generous 1$\frac{1}{2}$ cups
   long grain white rice
900 ml/1$\frac{1}{2}$ pints/3$\frac{3}{4}$ cups
   chicken stock
175 g/6 oz peeled cooked prawns
salt and pepper
12 cooked prawns in shells, with
   heads removed, to garnish

peeled prawns

prawns

garlic

chorizo

celery

rice

ground ginger

chilli powder

chicken thighs

chicken stock

red pepper

green pepper

onions

oil

1 Cut the chicken and chorizo into small, bite-sized pieces. Cut the celery and peppers into thin 5 cm/2 in strips.

2 Heat the oil in a very large frying pan or large saucepan and cook the chicken until golden. Remove with a slotted spoon and drain on kitchen paper. Cook the chorizo for 2 minutes and drain on kitchen paper.

3 Add the celery and peppers and cook for 3–4 minutes, until beginning to soften and turn golden. Drain on kitchen paper.

4 Add a little more oil to the pan, if necessary, and cook the onions and garlic for 3 minutes. Stir in the chilli powder and ginger and cook for a further 1 minute.

5 Add the rice; cook for 1 minute until it begins to look translucent. Stir in the stock, replace the chicken and bring to the boil. Cover and simmer for 12–15 minutes, stirring occasionally, until the rice is tender and the liquid absorbed. Add a little more water, if necessary, during cooking.

6 Gently stir the chorizo, peppers, celery and peeled prawns into the rice. Cook over a low heat, turning the mixture over with a large spoon, until piping hot. Adjust the seasoning and serve, garnished with the whole prawns.

Smoked Salmon Kedgeree

You could also try this recipe with grilled or poached fresh salmon: flake it and then use as for smoked salmon. For speed, buy frozen cooked rice, thaw 750 g/1¾ lb and omit step 1.

Serves 6

INGREDIENTS
275 g/10 oz/scant 1½ cups long
    grain white rice
25 g/1 oz/2 tbsp butter
30 ml/2 tbsp olive oil
1 onion, roughly chopped
2 garlic cloves, crushed
1 red pepper, seeded and
    roughly chopped
115 g/4 oz fine green beans, trimmed
    and halved
5 ml/1 tsp mild curry paste
115 g/4 oz peeled cooked prawns
175 g/6 oz smoked salmon or
    smoked salmon trimmings,
    roughly chopped
grated rind and juice of 1 lemon
60 ml/4 tbsp mixed chopped fresh
    dill and chives
salt and pepper
lemon wedges and fresh dill sprigs,
    to garnish
crusty bread, to serve

curry paste
garlic
fine green beans
butter
red pepper *onion*
chives
lemon *dill* *smoked salmon*

 olive oil
 rice
peeled prawns

1 Cook the rice in boiling, salted water until just tender, but still retaining a little bite (about 12 minutes). Rinse in boiling water and drain well.

2 Rinse out the pan and heat the butter and oil. Cook the onion, garlic, red pepper and beans for 5 minutes, or until beginning to soften.

3 Add the curry paste and cook for a further 1 minute. Add the prawns and rice and stir over a low heat until both are piping hot.

4 Add the smoked salmon and grated lemon rind and add lemon juice to taste. The salmon will begin to turn opaque. Adjust the seasoning and stir in the herbs. Serve immediately, garnished with lemon wedges and dill sprigs, with crusty bread.

Paella

Based on the classic Spanish recipe, a mixture of seafood is cooked with aromatic saffron rice.

Serves 6

INGREDIENTS
30 ml/2 tbsp olive oil
2 red peppers, seeded and
    roughly chopped
225 g/8 oz onions, roughly chopped
2 garlic cloves, crushed
115 g/4 oz streaky bacon,
    roughly chopped
350 g/12 oz/scant 1¾ cups long
    grain white rice
pinch of saffron strands
475 ml/16 fl oz/2 cups vegetable or
    chicken stock
300 ml/½ pint/1¼ cups dry
    white wine
350 g/12 oz ripe tomatoes
450 g/1 lb mixed cooked seafood,
    such as prawns, mussels and squid
115 g/4 oz/1 cup frozen peas, thawed
45 ml/3 tbsp chopped fresh parsley
salt and pepper
whole cooked prawns and mussels in
    their shells, to garnish

tomatoes   onions
                        garlic

white wine
mussels   peas
                    parsley

red peppers   streaky bacon

        saffron
prawns

vegetable
or chicken   cooked
stock   seafood

1 Heat the oil in a paella pan. Cook the peppers for 3 minutes or until beginning to soften; remove with a slotted spoon and drain on kitchen paper. Add a little more oil and cook the onions, garlic and bacon for about 5 minutes, or until the onions have softened slightly, stirring.

2 Add the rice; cook for 1 minute until it begins to turn translucent. Stir in the saffron, stock, wine and seasoning. Boil, then simmer, covered, for 12–15 minutes. Stir occasionally.

3 Meanwhile, quarter the tomatoes and scoop out the seeds. Roughly chop the flesh.

4 When the rice is cooked and most of the liquid has been absorbed, stir the tomatoes, seafood, peas and peppers into the mixture and heat gently, stirring occasionally, for about 5 minutes or until piping hot. Stir in the parsley and adjust the seasoning before serving, garnished with the prawns and mussels.

Smoky Bacon and Tomato Risotto

A classic risotto, with plenty of melting onions, smoked bacon and sun-dried tomatoes; you'll want to keep going back for more!

Serves 4

INGREDIENTS

8 sun-dried tomatoes in olive oil
275 g/10 oz rindless, good-quality
  smoked back bacon
75 g/3 oz/6 tbsp butter
450 g/1 lb/2 cups onions,
  roughly chopped
2 garlic cloves, crushed
350 g/12 oz/scant 1¾ cups risotto
  (arborio) rice
900 ml/1½ pints/3¾ cups hot
  vegetable stock
300 ml/½ pint/1¼ cups dry
  white wine
50 g/2 oz/⅔ cup Parmesan cheese,
  freshly grated
45 ml/3 tbsp mixed chopped fresh
  chives and flat leaf parsley
salt and pepper
lemon wedges, to serve
flat leaf parsley sprigs, to garnish

flat leaf parsley

onions

dry white wine

chives

garlic

lemon

vegetable stock

butter

Parmesan cheese

sun-dried tomatoes

smoked bacon

risotto rice

1 Drain the sun-dried tomatoes and reserve the oil. Roughly chop the tomatoes and set aside. Cut the smoked bacon into 2.5 cm/1 in strips.

2 Heat 15 ml/1 tbsp of the reserved oil in a large saucepan. Fry the bacon until well cooked and golden. Remove with a slotted spoon and drain on kitchen paper.

3 Add 25 g/1 oz of the butter to the pan and cook the onions and garlic over a medium heat for 10 minutes, until softened and golden brown.

4 Stir in the rice and cook for 1 minute until turning translucent. Mix together the stock and wine. Add a ladleful and cook gently, until absorbed.

5 Stir in more of the stock and wine mixture as each ladleful is absorbed; this should take 20–25 minutes. The risotto will turn thick and creamy and the rice should be tender but not sticky.

6 Just before serving, stir in the bacon, sun-dried tomatoes, half the Parmesan and herbs, and the remaining butter. Adjust the seasoning (remember that the bacon may be quite salty) and serve sprinkled with the remaining Parmesan and herbs. Garnish with parsley and serve with lemon wedges.

Lemony Couscous Salad

This is a wonderful salad to pile high and it tastes delicious served hot or cold. Add your favourite cheeses or meats, to give the salad a personal touch.

Serves 6

INGREDIENTS

275 g/10 oz/1²/₃ cups couscous
525 ml/18 fl oz/2¹/₄ cups hot
  vegetable stock
50 g/2 oz/4 tbsp butter
350 g/12 oz onions, roughly chopped
6 sun-dried tomatoes, finely chopped
75 ml/5 tbsp mixed chopped fresh
  chives and flat leaf parsley
350 g/12 oz chorizo sausages,
  roughly chopped
1 red pepper, seeded and
  roughly chopped
1 yellow pepper, seeded and
  roughly chopped
175 g/6 oz feta cheese, cubed
400 g/14 oz can artichoke hearts,
  drained and halved
grated rind and juice of 1 lemon
50 ml/2 fl oz/¹/₄ cup olive oil
5 ml/1 tsp caster sugar
salt and pepper

yellow pepper

vegetable stock

caster sugar

couscous

flat leaf parsley

red pepper

lemon

feta cheese

artichoke hearts

sun-dried tomatoes

chorizo sausages

olive oil

onions

chives

butter

1 Place the couscous in a large bowl and pour over the hot stock. Allow to stand until all the liquid has been absorbed, then gently fork the couscous to separate the grains. This can be prepared in the serving dish.

2 Heat the butter in a large frying pan and cook the onions for 5 minutes over a medium heat until softened and golden, stirring often.

3 Add half the onions to the couscous with the sun-dried tomatoes and 45 ml/3 tbsp of the herbs and mix until combined. Season well, transfer to a serving dish and set aside.

4 Add the chorizo and peppers to the remaining onions and cook over a medium heat for about 10–12 minutes, until the chorizo begins to brown and the peppers have softened. Cool the mixture slightly.

5 Toss the feta and artichokes into the chorizo mixture, season well and pile on top of the couscous. Allow to cool completely, if serving cold.

6 When ready to serve, mix together the lemon rind, 45 ml/3 tbsp of the lemon juice, the olive oil, sugar, remaining herbs and plenty of seasoning. Drizzle this dressing over the warm or cold salad to serve.

Thai Fried Noodles

A staple of day-to-day Thai life, this dish is often served on Thai street food stalls. It's an excellent way to make a little go a long way. If you like Thai fish sauce, sprinkle over a little extra at the table.

Serves 4

INGREDIENTS
175 g/6 oz ribbon rice noodles
30 ml/2 tbsp oil
2 garlic cloves, crushed
115 g/4 oz pork fillet, finely chopped
2 canned anchovy fillets, chopped
30 ml/2 tbsp lemon juice
45 ml/3 tbsp Thai fish sauce
15 ml/1 tbsp caster sugar
225 g/8 oz tofu (beancurd), cubed
2 eggs, beaten
75 g/3 oz peeled cooked prawns
115 g/4 oz/½ cup beansprouts
75 g/3 oz/½ cup unsalted
    roasted peanuts
75 ml/5 tbsp chopped
    fresh coriander
fresh coriander, to garnish (optional)
dried flaked chillies and Thai fish
    sauce, to serve

ribbon rice noodles

tofu

eggs

anchovy fillets

pork fillet

garlic

caster sugar

dried flaked chillies

beansprouts

Thai fish sauce

peanuts

lemon

oil

coriander

prawns

1 Soak the noodles in boiling water, according to the packet instructions; drain well.

2 Heat the oil in a wok or large frying pan and cook the garlic until golden. Add the pork and stir-fry until cooked and golden.

3 Reduce the heat slightly and stir in the anchovies, lemon juice, fish sauce and sugar. Bring to a gentle simmer.

4 Stir in the tofu, taking care not to break it up. Fold in the noodles gently until they are coated in the liquid.

5 Make a gap at the side of the pan and add the beaten eggs. Allow them to scramble slightly and then stir them into the noodles.

6 Stir in the prawns and most of the beansprouts, peanuts and coriander. Cook until piping hot. Serve the noodles topped with the remaining beansprouts, peanuts and coriander; sprinkled with a little dried flaked chillies and more fish sauce, to taste. Garnish with fresh coriander sprigs, if using.

Gingered Chicken Noodles

A blend of ginger, spices and coconut milk flavours this delicious supper dish, which is made in minutes. For a real oriental touch, add a little fish sauce to taste, just before serving.

Serves 4

INGREDIENTS

350 g/12 oz boneless, skinless
   chicken breasts
225 g/8 oz courgettes
275 g/10 oz aubergine
about 30 ml/2 tbsp oil
5 cm/2 in piece fresh root ginger,
   peeled and finely chopped
6 spring onions, sliced
10 ml/2 tsp Thai green curry paste
400 ml/14 fl oz/1²/₃ cups
   coconut milk
475 ml/16 fl oz/2 cups chicken stock
115 g/4 oz medium egg noodles
45 ml/3 tbsp chopped
   fresh coriander
15 ml/1 tbsp lemon juice
salt and pepper
chopped fresh coriander, to garnish

spring onions · chicken breasts · coriander · oil · chicken stock · aubergine · egg noodles · courgettes · lemon · Thai green curry paste · fresh root ginger · coconut milk

1 Cut the chicken into bite-sized pieces. Halve the courgettes lengthways and roughly chop them. Cut the aubergine into similarly sized pieces.

2 Heat the oil in a large saucepan and cook the chicken until golden. Remove with a slotted spoon and drain on kitchen paper.

3 Add a little more oil, if necessary, and cook the ginger and spring onions for 3 minutes. Add the courgettes and cook for 2–3 minutes, or until beginning to turn golden. Stir in the curry paste and cook for 1 minute.

4 Add the coconut milk, stock, aubergine and chicken and simmer for 10 minutes. Add the noodles and cook for a further 5 minutes, or until the chicken is cooked and the noodles are tender. Stir in the coriander and lemon juice and adjust the seasoning. Serve garnished with chopped fresh coriander.

Pork Chow Mein

A perfect speedy meal, this is flavoured with sesame oil for an authentic oriental taste.

Serves 4

INGREDIENTS

175 g/6 oz medium egg noodles
350 g/12 oz pork fillet
30 ml/2 tbsp sunflower oil
15 ml/1 tbsp sesame oil
2 garlic cloves, crushed
8 spring onions, sliced
1 red pepper, seeded and
　roughly chopped
1 green pepper, seeded and
　roughly chopped
30 ml/2 tbsp dark soy sauce
45 ml/3 tbsp dry sherry
175 g/6 oz/³/₄ cup beansprouts
45 ml/3 tbsp chopped fresh flat
　leaf parsley
15 ml/1 tbsp toasted sesame seeds

red pepper

medium egg noodles

green pepper

spring onions

flat leaf parsley

garlic

pork fillet

toasted sesame seeds

dark soy sauce

dry sherry

sesame oil

sunflower oil

beansprouts

1 Soak the noodles according to the packet instructions. Drain well.

2 Thinly slice the pork fillet. Heat the sunflower oil in a wok or large frying pan and cook the pork over a high heat until golden brown and cooked through.

3 Add the sesame oil to the pan, with the garlic, spring onions and peppers. Cook over a high heat for 3–4 minutes, or until beginning to soften.

4 Reduce the heat slightly and stir in the noodles, with the soy sauce and sherry. Stir-fry for 2 minutes. Add the beansprouts and cook for a further 1–2 minutes. If the noodles begin to stick, add a splash of water. Stir in the parsley and serve sprinkled with the sesame seeds.

Spicy Chicken Stir-fry

The chicken is marinated in an aromatic blend of spices and stir-fried with crisp vegetables. If you find it too spicy, serve with a spoonful of soured cream or yogurt. It's just as delicious hot or cold.

Serves 4

INGREDIENTS

2.5 ml/½ tsp each ground turmeric and ground ginger
5 ml/1 tsp each salt and ground black pepper
10 ml/2 tsp ground cumin
15 ml/1 tbsp ground coriander
15 ml/1 tbsp caster sugar
450 g/1 lb boneless, skinless chicken breast
1 bunch spring onions
4 celery sticks
2 red peppers, seeded
1 yellow pepper, seeded
175 g/6 oz courgettes
175 g/6 oz mangetouts or sugar snap peas
30 ml/2 tbsp sunflower oil
15 ml/1 tbsp lime juice
15 ml/1 tbsp clear honey

1 Mix together the turmeric, ginger, salt, pepper, cumin, coriander and sugar in a bowl until well combined.

2 Cut the chicken into bite-sized strips. Add to the spice mixture and stir to coat the chicken pieces thoroughly. Set aside.

yellow pepper

sunflower oil

lime

celery

courgettes

spring onions

red peppers

clear honey

ground coriander

salt

caster sugar

chicken breast

ground turmeric

ground ginger

ground black pepper

ground cumin

mangetouts

3 Prepare the vegetables. Cut the spring onions, celery and peppers into 5 cm/2 in long, thin strips. Cut the courgettes at a slight angle into thin rounds and top and tail the mangetouts or sugar snap peas.

4 Heat 30 ml/2 tbsp of oil in a large frying pan or wok. Stir-fry the chicken in batches until cooked through and golden brown, adding a little more oil if necessary. Remove from the pan and keep warm.

5 Add a little more oil to the pan and cook the onions, celery, peppers and courgettes over a medium heat for about 8–10 minutes, until beginning to soften and turn golden. Add the mange-touts or sugar snap peas and cook for a further 2 minutes.

6 Return the chicken to the pan, with the lime juice and honey. Cook for 2 minutes. Adjust the seasoning and serve immediately.

Beef Stir-fry with Crisp Parsnips

Wonderful crisp shreds of parsnip add extra crunchiness to this stir-fry. This is a great supper dish to share with friends.

Serves 4

INGREDIENTS
350 g/12 oz parsnips
450 g/1 lb rump steak
450 g/1 lb trimmed leeks
2 red peppers, seeded
350 g/12 oz courgettes
90 ml/6 tbsp vegetable oil
2 garlic cloves, crushed
45 ml/3 tbsp hoisin sauce
salt and pepper

red peppers

vegetable oil

hoisin sauce

leeks

rump steak

garlic

courgettes

parsnips

1 Peel the parsnips. Cut in half lengthways, place the flat surface on the board and cut into thin strips. Finely shred each piece. Rinse in cold water and drain thoroughly. Dry on kitchen paper if necessary.

2 Cut the steak into thin strips. Split the leeks in half lengthways and thickly slice at an angle. Roughly chop the peppers and thinly slice the courgettes.

3 Heat the oil in a wok or large frying pan. Fry the parsnips until crisp and golden. You may need to do this in batches, adding a little more oil if necessary. Remove with a slotted spoon and drain on kitchen paper.

4 Stir-fry the steak in the wok until golden and cooked through. You may need to do this in batches, adding more oil if necessary. Remove and drain on kitchen paper.

5 Stir-fry the garlic, leeks, peppers and courgettes for about 10 minutes, or until golden brown and beginning to soften but still retaining a little bite. Season the mixture well.

6 Return the meat to the pan with the hoisin sauce. Stir-fry for 2–3 minutes, or until piping hot. Adjust the seasoning and serve with the crisp parsnips piled on top.

Minted Lamb Stir-fry

Lamb and mint have a long-established partnership that works particularly well in this full-flavoured stir-fry. Serve with plenty of crusty bread.

Serves 2

INGREDIENTS

275 g/10 oz lamb neck fillet
30 ml/2 tbsp sunflower oil
10 ml/2 tsp sesame oil
1 onion, roughly chopped
2 garlic cloves, crushed
1 red chilli, seeded and
   finely chopped
75 g/3 oz fine green beans, halved
225 g/8 oz fresh spinach, shredded
30 ml/2 tbsp oyster sauce
30 ml/2 tbsp fish sauce
15 ml/1 tbsp lemon juice
5 ml/1 tsp caster sugar
45 ml/3 tbsp chopped fresh mint
salt and pepper
mint sprigs, to garnish
crusty bread, to serve

spinach

onions

lemon

garlic

red chilli   mint

lamb neck fillet

fine green beans

fish sauce

sesame oil

oyster sauce

sunflower oil

caster sugar

1 Trim the lamb of any excess fat and cut into thin slices. Heat the oils in a wok or large frying pan and cook the lamb over a high heat until browned. Remove with a slotted spoon and drain on kitchen paper.

2 Add the onion, garlic and chilli to the wok and cook for 2–3 minutes. Add the beans to the wok and stir-fry for 3 minutes.

3 Stir in the spinach with the browned meat, oyster sauce, fish sauce, lemon juice and sugar. Stir-fry for a further 3–4 minutes, or until the lamb is cooked through.

4 Sprinkle in the mint, adjust the seasoning and garnish with mint sprigs. Serve piping hot, with plenty of crusty bread to mop up all the juices.

Stir-fried Crispy Duck

This stir-fry would be delicious wrapped in flour tortillas or steamed Chinese pancakes, with a little extra warm plum sauce.

Serves 2

INGREDIENTS

275–350 g/10–12 oz boneless
    duck breast
30 ml/2 tbsp plain flour
60 ml/4 tbsp oil
1 bunch spring onions, halved
    lengthways and cut into
    5 cm/2 in strips
275 g/10 oz/2½ cups green cabbage,
    finely shredded
225 g/8 oz can water chestnuts,
    drained and sliced
50 g/2 oz/⅓ cup unsalted
    cashew nuts
115 g/4 oz cucumber, cut into strips
45 ml/3 tbsp plum sauce
15 ml/1 tbsp light soy sauce
salt and pepper
sliced spring onions, to garnish

plum sauce   cashew nuts   oil

water   plain   light soy
chestnuts   flour   sauce

green
cabbage   spring
          onions
duck
breast

      cucumber

1 Trim a little of the fat from the duck and thinly slice the meat. Season the flour well and use it to coat each piece of duck.

2 Heat the oil in a wok or large frying pan and cook the duck over a high heat until golden and crisp. Keep stirring to prevent the duck from sticking. Remove with a slotted spoon and drain on kitchen paper. You may need to do this in batches.

3 Add the spring onions to the pan and cook for 2 minutes. Stir in the cabbage and cook for 5 minutes, or until softened and golden.

4 Return the duck to the pan with the water chestnuts, cashews and cucumber. Stir-fry for 2 minutes. Add the plum sauce and soy sauce with plenty of seasoning, and heat for 2 minutes. Serve piping hot, garnished with sliced spring onions.

Sweet-and-Sour Pork Stir-fry

This is a great idea for a quick family supper. Remember to cut the carrots into thin strips so that they cook in time.

Serves 4

INGREDIENTS
450 g/1 lb pork fillet (tenderloin)
30 ml/2 tbsp plain flour
45 ml/3 tbsp oil
1 onion, roughly chopped
1 garlic clove, crushed
1 green pepper, seeded and sliced
350 g/12 oz carrots, cut into strips
225 g/8 oz can bamboo
    shoots, drained
15 ml/1 tbsp white wine vinegar
15 ml/1 tbsp soft brown sugar
10 ml/2 tsp tomato purée
30 ml/2 tbsp light soy sauce
salt and pepper

light soy sauce

white wine vinegar

soft brown sugar

oil

bamboo shoots

plain flour

carrots

onion

green pepper

tomato purée

garlic

pork fillet

1 Thinly slice the pork. Season the flour and toss the pork in it to coat.

2 Heat the oil in a wok or large frying pan and cook the pork over a medium heat for about 5 minutes, until golden and cooked through. Remove with a slotted spoon and drain on kitchen paper. You may need to do this in batches.

3 Add the onion and garlic to the pan and cook for 3 minutes. Stir in the pepper and carrots and stir-fry over a high heat for 6–8 minutes, or until beginning to soften slightly.

4 Return the meat to the pan with the bamboo shoots. Add the remaining ingredients with 120 ml/4 fl oz/½ cup water and bring to the boil. Simmer gently for 2–3 minutes, or until piping hot. Adjust the seasoning, if necessary, and serve immediately.

Gingered Seafood Stir-fry

A refreshing summer supper, served with plenty of crusty bread to mop up the juices and a glass of chilled dry white wine. It would also make a great starter for four people.

Serves 2

INGREDIENTS

15 ml/1 tbsp sunflower oil
5 ml/1 tsp sesame oil
2.5 cm/1 in piece fresh root ginger, peeled and finely chopped
1 bunch spring onions, sliced
1 red pepper, seeded and finely chopped
115 g/4 oz small "queen" scallops
8 large uncooked prawns, shelled
115 g/4 oz squid rings
15 ml/1 tbsp lime juice
15 ml/1 tbsp light soy sauce
60 ml/4 tbsp coconut milk
salt and pepper
mixed salad leaves and crusty bread, to serve

salad leaves   *spring onions*   *uncooked prawns*   *"queen" scallops*   *fresh root ginger*   *lime*   *light soy sauce*   *red pepper*   *squid rings*   *sesame oil*   *sunflower oil*   *coconut milk*

1 Heat the oils in a wok or large frying pan and cook the ginger and spring onions for 2–3 minutes, or until golden. Stir in the red pepper and cook for a further 3 minutes.

2 Add the scallops, prawns and squid rings and cook over a medium heat for about 3 minutes, until the seafood is just cooked.

3 Stir in the lime juice, soy sauce and coconut milk. Simmer, uncovered, for 2 minutes, until the juices begin to thicken slightly.

4 Season well. Arrange the salad leaves on serving plates and spoon over the seafood mixture with the juices. Serve with plenty of crusty bread to mop up the juices.

Vegetable Stir-fry with Eggs

A perfect family supper dish, this is very easy to prepare. Serve with plenty of crusty bread: Italian ciabatta is particularly good. Ask your butcher to cut the ham thickly in one piece.

Serves 4

INGREDIENTS
30 ml/2 tbsp olive oil
1 onion, roughly chopped
2 garlic cloves, crushed
175 g/6 oz cooked ham
225 g/8 oz courgettes
1 red pepper, seeded and
  thinly sliced
1 yellow pepper, seeded and
  thinly sliced
10 ml/2 tsp paprika
400 g/14 oz can chopped tomatoes
15 ml/1 tbsp sun-dried tomato paste
  or tomato purée
4 eggs
115 g/4 oz Cheddar cheese, grated
salt and pepper
crusty bread, to serve

yellow pepper

tomato purée

paprika

red pepper

Cheddar cheese

garlic

cooked ham

onion

courgettes

eggs

olive oil

chopped tomatoes

1 Heat the oil in a deep frying pan and cook the onion and garlic for 4 minutes, or until beginning to soften.

2 Meanwhile, cut the ham and courgettes into 5 cm/2 in long batons or strips. Set the ham aside.

3 Add the courgettes and peppers to the onion and cook over a medium heat for 3–4 minutes, or until beginning to soften.

4 Stir in the paprika, tomatoes, sun-dried tomato paste or purée, ham and seasoning. Bring to the boil and simmer gently for 15 minutes, or until the vegetables are just tender.

5 Reduce the heat to a low setting. Make four wells in the tomato mixture, break an egg into each and season. Cook over a gentle heat until the egg white begins to set.

6 Preheat the grill to hot. Sprinkle over the cheese. Protect the pan handle with foil. Cook under the grill for about 5 minutes until the cheese is golden and the eggs are lightly set. Serve at once with plenty of crusty bread.

Pan Haggerty

Use a firm-fleshed potato, such as Romano or Maris Piper, which will hold its shape when cooked. For a change, try adding chopped ham or salami between the layers.

Serves 2

INGREDIENTS
1 large onion
450 g/1 lb potatoes
30 ml/2 tbsp olive oil
25 g/1 oz/2 tbsp butter
2 garlic cloves, crushed
115 g/4 oz/1 cup mature Cheddar
    cheese, grated
45 ml/3 tbsp chopped fresh chives
salt and pepper
chopped fresh chives, to garnish

potatoes   olive oil

butter   onion

garlic

Cheddar cheese

chives

1 Halve and thinly slice the onion. Peel and thinly slice the potatoes.

2 Heat the oil and butter in a large heavy-based or non-stick frying pan. Remove from the heat and cover the base with a layer of potatoes, followed by layers of onion, garlic, cheese, chives and seasoning.

3 Continue layering, ending with cheese. Cover and cook over a gentle heat for about 30 minutes, or until the potatoes and onion are tender.

4 Preheat the grill to hot. Uncover the pan, protect the pan handle with foil, and brown the top under the grill. Serve straight from the pan, sprinkled with extra chives to garnish.

Tuna Frittata

This is the ultimate meal in a pan. For a stronger cheese flavour, why not try a creamy goat's cheese instead of the soft cheese?

Serves 2-3

INGREDIENTS
25 g/1 oz/2 tbsp butter
15 ml/1 tbsp olive oil
1 onion, finely chopped
175 g/6 oz courgettes, halved
  lengthways and sliced
75 g/3 oz/scant 1¼ cups brown-cap
  mushrooms, sliced
50 g/2 oz asparagus tips
4 eggs, beaten
75 g/3 oz/⅜ cup soft cheese
30 ml/2 tbsp chopped fresh thyme
200 g/7 oz can tuna in brine, drained
  and roughly flaked
115 g/4 oz peeled cooked prawns
salt and pepper

onion

tuna

brown-cap
mushrooms

soft cheese

eggs

thyme

prawns

olive oil

asparagus
tips

courgettes

1 Heat the butter and oil in a medium-size, preferably non-stick, frying pan. Cook the onion for 3 minutes. Add the courgettes, mushrooms and asparagus and cook for a further 10 minutes, or until beginning to soften and brown.

2 Beat together the eggs, soft cheese, thyme and plenty of seasoning until well combined.

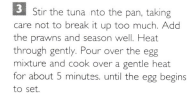

3 Stir the tuna into the pan, taking care not to break it up too much. Add the prawns and season well. Heat through gently. Pour over the egg mixture and cook over a gentle heat for about 5 minutes, until the egg begins to set.

4 Push the egg away from the sides to allow uncooked egg to run on to the pan. Preheat the grill to medium. Protect the pan handle with foil and place under the grill to set and brown the surface. Serve cut in wedges.

Spicy Sausage, Caramelized Onion and Cheese Tortilla

A colourful, Spanish-style omelette, which is delicious served hot or cold, cut into wedges, with a tomato salad.

Serves 4-6

INGREDIENTS

675 g/1½ lb potatoes, peeled
275 g/10 oz onions
175 g/6 oz chorizo or spicy sausages
75 ml/5 tbsp olive oil
4 eggs, beaten
30 ml/2 tbsp chopped fresh parsley
115 g/4 oz/1 cup Cheddar
    cheese, grated
salt and pepper
fresh flat leaf parsley, to garnish

potatoes

olive oil

Cheddar cheese

chorizo or spicy sausages

eggs

parsley

onions

1 Thinly slice the potatoes. Halve and thinly slice the onions. Thinly slice the chorizo or spicy sausages.

2 Heat 15 ml/1 tbsp of oil in a non-stick frying pan, about 20 cm/8 in in diameter, and fry the sliced sausage until golden brown and cooked through. Drain on kitchen paper.

3 Add a further 30 ml/2 tbsp oil and fry the potatoes and onions for 2–3 minutes, turning frequently (the pan will be very full). Cover tightly and cook over a gentle heat for about 30 minutes, turning occasionally, until softened and slightly golden.

4 Mix the beaten eggs in a bowl, with the parsley, cheese, sausage and plenty of seasoning. Gently stir in the potatoes and onions until coated, taking care not to break up the potatoes too much.

5 Wipe out the pan with kitchen paper and heat the remaining 30 ml/2 tbsp oil. Add the mixture and cook over a low heat, until the egg begins to set. Use a palette knife to prevent the tortilla from sticking to the sides.

6 Preheat the grill to hot. When the base has set (after about 5 minutes), protect the pan handle with foil and place under the grill until set and golden. Turn out, garnish with flat leaf parsley and cut into wedges to serve.

Vegetable Hot-pot with Cheese Triangles

Use a selection of your favourite vegetables, so long as the overall weight remains the same. Firm vegetables may need a little longer cooking.

Serves 6

INGREDIENTS
30 ml/2 tbsp oil
2 garlic cloves, crushed
1 onion, roughly chopped
5 ml/1 tsp mild chilli powder
450 g/1 lb potatoes, peeled and
   roughly chopped
450 g/1 lb celeriac, peeled and
   roughly chopped
350 g/12 oz carrots, roughly
   chopped
350 g/12 oz trimmed leeks,
   roughly chopped
225 g/8 oz/3 cups brown-cap
   mushrooms, halved
20 ml/4 tsp plain flour
600 ml/1 pint/2¹/₂ cups
   vegetable stock
400 g/14 oz can chopped tomatoes
15 ml/1 tbsp tomato purée
30 ml/2 tbsp chopped fresh thyme
400 g/14 oz can kidney beans,
   drained and rinsed
salt and pepper

FOR THE TOPPING
115 g/4 oz/8 tbsp butter
225 g/8 oz/2 cups self-raising flour
115 g/4 oz vegetarian Cheddar
   cheese, grated
30 ml/2 tbsp snipped fresh chives
about 75 ml/5 tbsp milk
fresh thyme sprigs,
   to garnish (optional)

1 Preheat the oven to 180°C/350°F/ Gas 4. Heat the oil in a large flameproof casserole and fry the garlic and onion for 5 minutes, or until beginning to brown. Stir in the chilli powder and cook for a further 1 minute.

2 Add the potatoes, celeriac, carrots, leeks and mushrooms. Cook for 3–4 minutes. Stir in the flour and cook for a further 1 minute.

3 Gradually stir in the stock with the tomatoes, tomato purée, thyme and plenty of seasoning. Bring to the boil, stirring. Cover and cook in the oven for 30 minutes.

4 Meanwhile, make the topping. Rub the butter into the flour, stir in half the cheese with the chives and plenty of seasoning. Add just enough milk to bind the mixture to a smooth dough.

onion

brown-cap mushrooms

celeriac

vegetable stock

tomato purée

thyme

garlic

self-raising flour

potatoes

leeks

milk

chives

chilli powder

carrots

leeks

plain flour

vegetarian Cheddar cheese

butter

chopped tomatoes

kidney beans

oil

5 Roll out the dough until it is about 2.5 cm/1 in thick and cut into 12 triangles. Brush with a little milk.

6 Remove the casserole from the oven, add the beans and stir to combine. Place the triangles on top, overlapping them slightly, and sprinkle with the remaining cheese. Return to the oven, uncovered, for 20–25 minutes, or until golden brown and cooked through. Serve, garnished with fresh thyme sprigs, if using.

Curried Spinach and Chick-peas

Try serving this with a spoonful of natural yogurt and accompany it with naan bread, for a complete and very tasty meal.

Serves 6

INGREDIENTS
45 ml/3 tbsp vegetable oil
2 garlic cloves, crushed
1 onion, roughly chopped
30 ml/2 tbsp medium curry paste
15 ml/1 tbsp black mustard seeds
450 g/1 lb/4 cups potatoes, cut into
    small cubes
450 g/1 lb frozen leaf
    spinach, thawed
400 g/14 oz can chick-peas, drained
225 g/8 oz/2 cups halloumi or
    paneer cheese, cubed
15 ml/1 tbsp lime juice
salt and pepper
fresh coriander, to garnish

lime

chick-peas

spinach

garlic

onion

halloumi cheese

black mustard seeds

potatoes

medium curry paste

vegetable oil

1 Heat the oil in a large, heavy-based saucepan and cook the garlic and onion over a medium heat for about 5 minutes, or until the onion begins to soften, stirring frequently. Add the curry paste and mustard seeds and cook the mixture for 1 minute.

2 Add the potatoes, with 475 ml/16 fl oz/2 cups water. Bring to the boil and simmer gently, uncovered, for 20–25 minutes, until the potatoes are almost tender and most of the liquid has evaporated, stirring occasionally.

3 Meanwhile, place the thawed spinach in a sieve and press out as much liquid as possible. Chop roughly.

4 Stir in the spinach and chick-peas and cook for a further 5 minutes, or until the potatoes are tender. Add a little more water, if necessary (it should not be too wet). Stir frequently to prevent the mixture from sticking. Stir in the cheese and lime juice, adjust the seasoning and serve, garnished with fresh coriander.

Sun-dried Tomato and Parmesan Carbonara

Ingredients for this recipe can easily be doubled up to serve four. Why not try it with plenty of garlic bread and a big green salad?

Serves 2

INGREDIENTS

175 g/6 oz tagliatelle
50 g/2 oz sun-dried tomatoes in olive oil, drained
2 eggs, beaten
150 ml/¼ pint/⅔ cup double cream
15 ml/1 tbsp wholegrain mustard
50 g/2 oz/⅔ cup Parmesan cheese, freshly grated
12 fresh basil leaves, shredded
salt and pepper
fresh basil leaves, to garnish
crusty bread, to serve

1 Cook the pasta in boiling, salted water until it is just tender but still retains a little bite (*al dente*).

fresh basil

Parmesan cheese

sun-dried tomatoes

tagliatelle

wholegrain mustard

double cream

eggs

2 Meanwhile, cut the sun-dried tomatoes into small pieces.

3 Beat together the eggs, cream and mustard with plenty of seasoning until well combined.

4 Drain the pasta and immediately return to the hot saucepan with the cream mixture, sun-dried tomatoes, Parmesan cheese and shredded fresh basil. Return to a very low heat for 1 minute, stirring gently until the mixture thickens slightly. Adjust the seasoning and serve immediately, garnished with basil leaves. Serve with plenty of crusty bread.

Oriental Fried Rice

This is a great way to use leftover cooked rice. Make sure the rice is very cold before attempting to fry it: warm rice will become soggy. Some supermarkets sell frozen cooked rice.

Serves 4-6

INGREDIENTS

75 ml/5 tbsp oil
115 g/4 oz shallots, halved and
    thinly sliced
3 garlic cloves, crushed
1 red chilli, seeded and
    finely chopped
6 spring onions, finely chopped
1 red pepper, seeded and
    finely chopped
225 g/8 oz white cabbage, finely
    shredded
175 g/6 oz cucumber,
    finely chopped
50 g/2 oz/¹/₂ cup frozen peas, thawed
3 eggs, beaten
5 ml/1 tsp tomato purée
30 ml/2 tbsp lime juice
1.5 ml/¹/₄ tsp Tabasco sauce
675 g/1¹/₂ lb cooked white rice,
    cooled (equivalent to
    225 g/8 oz raw weight)
115 g/4 oz/²/₃ cup cashew nuts,
    roughly chopped
about 30 ml/2 tbsp chopped
    fresh coriander
salt and pepper

1 Heat the oil in a large non-stick frying pan or wok and cook the shallots until very crisp and golden. Remove with a slotted spoon and drain on kitchen paper.

2 Add the garlic and chilli and cook for 1 minute. Add the spring onions and pepper and cook for 3–4 minutes, or until beginning to soften.

3 Add the cabbage, cucumber and peas and cook for a further 2 minutes.

spring onions

coriander

red chilli

cucumber

Tabasco sauce

white cabbage

garlic

oil

cooked rice

red pepper

eggs

peas

lime

shallots

cashew nuts

tomato purée

4 Make a gap and add the beaten eggs. Scramble the eggs, stirring occasionally, and then stir them into the vegetables.

5 Add the tomato purée, lime juice and Tabasco and stir to combine.

6 Increase the heat and add the rice, cashew nuts and coriander with plenty of seasoning. Stir-fry for 3–4 minutes, until piping hot. Serve garnished with the crisp shallots and extra fresh coriander, if you like.

Leek, Mushroom and Lemon Risotto

A delicious risotto, packed full of flavour, this is a great recipe for an informal supper with friends.

Serves 4

INGREDIENTS

225 g/8 oz trimmed leeks
225 g/8 oz/generous 3 cups brown-cap mushrooms
30 ml/2 tbsp olive oil
3 garlic cloves, crushed
75 g/3 oz/6 tbsp butter
1 large onion, roughly chopped
350 g/12 oz/scant 1¾ cups risotto (arborio) rice
1.2 litres/2 pints/5 cups hot vegetable stock
grated rind and juice of 1 lemon
50 g/2 oz/⅔ cup Parmesan cheese, freshly grated
60 ml/4 tbsp mixed chopped fresh chives and flat leaf parsley
salt and pepper
lemon wedges, to serve

leeks

vegetable stock

Parmesan cheese

lemon

butter

risotto rice

onion

garlic

brown-cap mushrooms

olive oil

parsley

chives

1 Wash the leeks well. Slice in half, lengthways and roughly chop. Wipe the mushrooms with kitchen paper and roughly chop.

2 Heat the oil in a large saucepan and cook the garlic for 1 minute. Add the leeks, mushrooms and plenty of seasoning and cook over a medium heat for about 10 minutes, or until softened and browned. Remove from the pan and set aside.

3 Add 25 g/1 oz of the butter to the pan and cook the onion over a medium heat for about 5 minutes until softened and golden.

4 Stir in the rice and cook for 1 minute until the grains begin to look translucent and are coated in the fat. Add a ladleful of stock to the pan and cook gently, stirring occasionally, until the liquid is absorbed.

5 Stir in more liquid as each ladleful is absorbed; this should take 20–25 minutes. The risotto will turn thick and creamy and the rice should be tender but not sticky.

6 Just before serving, stir in the leeks, mushrooms, remaining butter, grated lemon rind and 45 ml/3 tbsp of the juice, half the Parmesan and herbs. Adjust the seasoning and serve, sprinkled with the remaining Parmesan and herbs. Serve with lemon wedges.

Ratatouille Couscous

A rich mixture of courgettes, aubergine, peppers and tomatoes on a light, lemony couscous: serve plenty of grated cheese to melt on the ratatouille.

Serves 6

INGREDIENTS
30 ml/2 tbsp olive oil
1 onion, roughly chopped
2 garlic cloves, crushed
1 red pepper, seeded and
    roughly chopped
350 g/12 oz courgettes, thickly sliced
275 g/10 oz aubergine,
    roughly chopped
450 g/1 lb plum tomatoes,
    roughly chopped
30 ml/2 tbsp sun-dried tomato paste
60 ml/4 tbsp mixed chopped fresh
    basil, parsley and thyme
salt and pepper

FOR THE COUSCOUS
550 ml/18 fl oz/2¼ cups hot
    vegetable stock
pinch of saffron strands
275 g/10 oz/scant 1¾ cups couscous
grated rind and juice of 1 lemon
50 ml/2 fl oz/¼ cup olive oil
45 ml/3 tbsp chopped fresh parsley
175 g/6 oz Cheddar cheese, grated

1 Heat the oil in a large saucepan and cook the onion and garlic for 5 minutes, until beginning to soften but not colour.

2 Add the pepper, courgettes and aubergine and stir-fry over a medium heat for 5 minutes.

3 Add the tomatoes, tomato paste, mixed herbs and plenty of seasoning. Cover and cook over a medium heat for about 20 minutes or until tender, thick and juicy. Simmer, uncovered, for a few minutes if the mixture is too wet.

couscous

sun-dried tomato paste

saffron

aubergine

garlic

thyme

red pepper

vegetable stock

basil

olive oil

courgettes

lemon

onion

Cheddar cheese

plum tomatoes

parsley

4 Meanwhile, pour the hot stock over the saffron and leave to infuse for 5 minutes. Place the couscous in a large bowl and pour over the stock. Allow to stand until all the liquid is absorbed. Fork the grains to separate them.

5 Whisk together the grated rind and juice of the lemon, olive oil, parsley and plenty of seasoning. Pour over the couscous and stir in with a fork until combined. Transfer to a serving dish.

6 Adjust the ratatouille seasoning. Spoon it over the couscous and sprinkle with the grated cheese to serve.

Peanut Noodles

Add any of your favourite vegetables to this recipe, which is quick to make for a great mid-week supper – and increase the chilli, if you can take the heat!

Serves 4

INGREDIENTS
200 g/7 oz medium egg noodles
30 ml/2 tbsp olive oil
2 garlic cloves, crushed
1 large onion, roughly chopped
1 red pepper, seeded and
    roughly chopped
1 yellow pepper, seeded and
    roughly chopped
350 g/12 oz courgettes,
    roughly chopped
150 g/5 oz/generous ¾ cup
    roasted unsalted peanuts,
    roughly chopped

FOR THE DRESSING
50 ml/2 fl oz/¼ cup good-quality
    olive oil
grated rind and juice of 1 lemon
1 red chilli, seeded and
    finely chopped
45 ml/3 tbsp chopped fresh chives
15–30 ml/1–2 tbsp balsamic vinegar
salt and pepper
chopped fresh chives, to garnish

red pepper   balsamic   garlic
              vinegar

red
chilli

courgettes   peanuts

chives

onion

yellow pepper

egg
noodles

olive
oil

lemon

1 Soak the noodles according to the packet instructions and drain well.

2 Meanwhile, heat the oil in a very large frying pan or wok and cook the garlic and onion for 3 minutes, or until beginning to soften. Add the peppers and courgettes and cook for a further 15 minutes over a medium heat until beginning to soften and brown. Add the peanuts and cook for a further 1 minute.

3 Whisk together the olive oil, grated rind and 45 ml/3 tbsp lemon juice, the chilli, chives, plenty of seasoning and balsamic vinegar to taste.

4 Toss the noodles into the vegetables and stir-fry to heat through. Add the dressing, stir to coat and serve immediately, garnished with chopped fresh chives.

Potato, Parsnip and Cumin Tortilla

Three great flavours come together: use a good mature Cheddar to balance them.

Serves 4-6

INGREDIENTS

60 ml/4 tbsp olive oil
500 g/1¼ lb potatoes, thinly sliced
225 g/8 oz parsnips, thinly sliced
275 g/10 oz onions, halved and
  thinly sliced
4 eggs, beaten
10 ml/2 tsp cumin seeds
115 g/4 oz/1 cup mature Cheddar
  cheese, grated
salt and pepper
fresh flat leaf parsley, to garnish

cumin seeds

parsnips

onions

potatoes

Cheddar cheese

eggs

parsley

olive oil

1 Heat 30 ml/2 tbsp of the oil in a frying pan, preferably non-stick, about 20 cm/8 in in diameter. Fry the potatoes, parsnips and onions for 2–3 minutes, turning occasionally; the pan will be quite full. Cover tightly and cook over a gentle heat for about 30 minutes, turning occasionally, until softened and slightly golden.

2 Place the beaten eggs in a bowl, with the cumin, cheese and plenty of seasoning. Stir in the potatoes, parsnips and onions, until coated, taking care not to break up the potatoes.

3 Heat a further 30 ml/2 tbsp olive oil in the pan and add the potato mixture. Cook over a low heat, until the egg begins to set. Use a palette knife to prevent the tortilla from sticking to the sides of the pan.

4 Preheat the grill to hot. When the base has set, after about 5 minutes, protect the pan handle with foil, and place under the grill until set and golden. Turn out and cut into wedges to serve, garnished with flat leaf parsley.

Spiced Tofu Stir-fry

You could add any quickly cooked vegetable to this stir-fry – try mangetouts, sugar snap peas, leeks or thin slices of carrot.

Serves 4

INGREDIENTS

10 ml/2 tsp ground cumin
15 ml/1 tbsp paprika
5 ml/1 tsp ground ginger
good pinch of cayenne pepper
15 ml/1 tbsp caster sugar
275 g/10 oz tofu (beancurd)
60 ml/4 tbsp oil
2 garlic cloves, crushed
1 bunch spring onions, sliced
1 red pepper, seeded and sliced
1 yellow pepper, seeded and sliced
225 g/8 oz/generous 3 cups
    brown-cap mushrooms, halved or
    quartered, if necessary
1 large courgette, sliced
115 g/4 oz fine green beans, halved
50 g/2 oz/scant $\frac{1}{2}$ cup pine nuts
15 ml/1 tbsp lime juice
15 ml/1 tbsp clear honey
salt and pepper

tofu
paprika
pine nuts
red pepper
cayenne pepper
spring onions
ground cumin
clear honey
oil
ground ginger
lime
garlic
yellow pepper
fine green beans
courgette
caster sugar
brown-cap mushrooms

1 Mix together the cumin, paprika, ginger, cayenne and sugar with plenty of seasoning. Cut the tofu into cubes and coat them in the spice mixture.

2 Heat some oil in a wok or large frying pan. Cook the tofu over a high heat for 3–4 minutes, turning occasionally (take care not to break up the tofu too much). Remove with a slotted spoon. Wipe out the pan with kitchen paper.

3 Add a little more oil to the pan and cook the garlic and spring onions for 3 minutes. Add the remaining vegetables and cook over a medium heat for 6 minutes, or until beginning to soften and turn golden. Season well.

4 Return the tofu to the pan with the pine nuts, lime juice and honey. Heat through and serve immediately.

Oven-baked Vegetables with Cheese and Olives

Finishing the vegetables in the oven really brings out their natural flavours. Why not try adding fennel, carrot or mushrooms?

Serves 6

INGREDIENTS

4 small onions, about 450 g/1 lb
   total weight
2 red peppers, seeded
2 yellow peppers, seeded
275 g/10 oz aubergine
450 g/1 lb courgettes
900 g/2 lb butternut squash
   or pumpkin
olive oil
8 whole garlic cloves, unpeeled
30 ml/2 tbsp balsamic vinegar
24 black olives, pitted
225 g/8 oz Roquefort or other blue
   cheese, sliced
salt and freshly ground black pepper
crusty bread, to serve

olive oil

garlic

courgettes

black olives

butternut squash

balsamic vinegar

red peppers

blue cheese

aubergine

onions

yellow peppers

1 Preheat the oven to 220°C/425°F/ Gas 7. Peel and quarter the onions. Roughly chop the peppers, aubergine and courgettes into similarly sized pieces. Peel the butternut squash or pumpkin, remove the seeds and roughly chop the flesh.

2 Heat 60 ml/4 tbsp of oil in a large, shallow flameproof casserole or roasting tin. Add all the vegetables and the unpeeled garlic and fry over a medium heat for 10 minutes, or until beginning to brown and char. Season well.

3 Place the vegetables in the oven, uncovered, and cook, stirring occasionally, for 50 minutes, or until tender and well browned. Stir in the balsamic vinegar, with 30 ml/2 tbsp of olive oil and plenty of seasoning.

4 Stir in the olives and lay the slices of cheese over the vegetables. Return to the oven for 5 minutes, until the cheese begins to melt. Serve with plenty of crusty bread to mop up the juices.

INDEX